ROCKS AND MINERALS

Britannica Illustrated Science Library

Encyclopædia Britannica, Inc.
Chicago ■ London ■ New Delhi ■ Paris ■ Seoul ■ Sydney ■ Taipei ■ Tokyo

Britannica Illustrated Science Library

Idea and Concept of This Work: Editorial Sol 90

Project Management: Fabián Cassan

Photo Credits: Corbis, ESA, Getty Images, Graphic News, NASA, National Geographic, Science Photo Library

Illustrators: Guido Arroyo, Pablo Aschei, Gustavo J. Caironi, Hernán Cañellas, Leonardo César, José Luis Corsetti, Vanina Farías, Joana Garrido, Celina Hilbert, Isidro López, Diego Martín, Jorge Martínez, Marco Menco, Ala de Mosca, Diego Mourelos, Eduardo Pérez, Javier Pérez, Ariel Piroyansky, Ariel Roldán, Marcel Socías, Néstor Taylor, Trebol Animation, Juan Venegas, Coralia Vignau, 3DN, 3DOM studio, Jorge Ivanovich, Fernando Ramallo, Constanza Vicco, Diego Mourelos

Composition and Pre-press Services: Editorial Sol 90

Translation Services and Index: Publication Services, Inc.

Britannica Illustrated Science Library Staff

Editorial
Michael Levy, *Executive Editor, Core Editorial*
John Rafferty, *Associate Editor, Earth Sciences*
William L. Hosch, *Associate Editor, Mathematics and Computers*
Kara Rogers, *Associate Editor, Life Sciences*
Rob Curley, *Senior Editor, Science and Technology*
David Hayes, *Special Projects Editor*

Art and Composition
Steven N. Kapusta, *Director*
Carol A. Gaines, *Composition Supervisor*
Christine McCabe, *Senior Illustrator*

Media Acquisition
Kathy Nakamura, *Manager*

Copy Department
Sylvia Wallace, *Director*
Julian Ronning, *Supervisor*

Information Management and Retrieval
Sheila Vasich, *Information Architect*

Production Control
Marilyn L. Barton

Manufacturing
Kim Gerber, *Director*

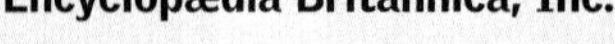

Encyclopædia Britannica, Inc.

Jacob E. Safra, *Chairman of the Board*

Jorge Aguilar-Cauz, *President*

Michael Ross, *Senior Vice President, Corporate Development*

Dale H. Hoiberg, *Senior Vice President and Editor*

Marsha Mackenzie, *Director of Production*

International Standard Book Number (set):
978-1-59339-382-3
International Standard Book Number (volume):
978-1-59339-396-0
Britannica Illustrated Science Library:
Rocks and Minerals 2008

Printed in China

www.britannica.com

Rocks and Minerals

Contents

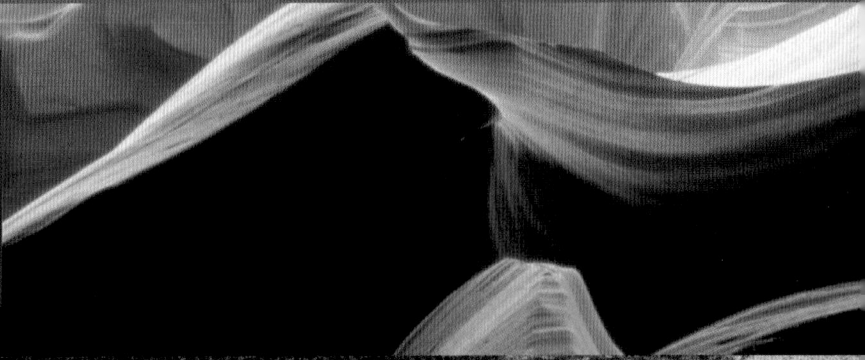

Dynamics of the Earth's Crust
Page 6

Minerals
Page 18

Formation and Transformation of Rocks
Page 40

Classes of Rocks
Page 60

Use of Rocks and Minerals
Page 76

PHOTOGRAPH ON PAGE 1
A stone with a blue opal in its center is a product of time, since it forms over millions of years.

Memory of the Planet

Rocks, like airplane flight recorders, store in their interior very useful information about what has happened in the past. Whether forming caves in the middle of mountains, mixed among folds, or lying at the bottom of lakes and oceans, stones are everywhere, and they hold clues to the past. By studying rocks, we can reconstruct the history of the Earth. Even the most insignificant rocks can tell stories about other times, because rocks have been around since the beginning of the universe. They were part of the cloud of dust and gases that revolved around the Sun over four billion years ago. Rocks have been

THE MONK'S HOUSE
This orthodox monk lives in a volcanic cave, very close to the 11 Christian churches located in the Ethiopian town of Lalibela.

silent witnesses to the cataclysms our planet has experienced. They know the cold of the glacial era, the intense heat of the Earth's interior, and the fury of the oceans. They store much information about how external agents, such as wind, rain, ice, and temperature changes, have been altering the planet's surface for millions of years.

For ancient civilizations, stones symbolized eternity. This idea has persisted throughout time because stones endure, but they are recycled time and again. Fifty million years from now, nothing will be as we now know it—not the Andes, nor the Himalayas, nor the ice of Antarctica, nor the Sahara Desert. Weathering and erosion, though slow, will never stop. This should free us from any illusion of the immortality of the Earth's features. What will everything be like in the future? We don't know. The only sure thing is that there will be rocks. Only stones will remain, and their chemical composition, shape, and texture will provide clues about previous geological events and about what the Earth's surface was like in the past. In the pages of this book, illustrated with stunning images, you will find invaluable information about the language of rocks and natural forces in general. You will also learn to identify the most important minerals, know their physical and chemical properties, and discover the environments in which they form.

Did you know that the Earth's crust and its oceans are sources of useful and essential minerals for human beings? Coal, petroleum, and natural gas found in the crust allow us to travel and to heat our homes. Furthermore, practically all the products that surround us have elements provided by rocks and minerals. For example, aluminum is used to produce beverage cans; copper is used in electric cables; and titanium, mixed with other durable metals, is used in the construction of spacecraft. We invite you to enjoy this book. It is full of interesting and worthwhile information. Don't miss out on it!

Dynamics of the Earth's Crust

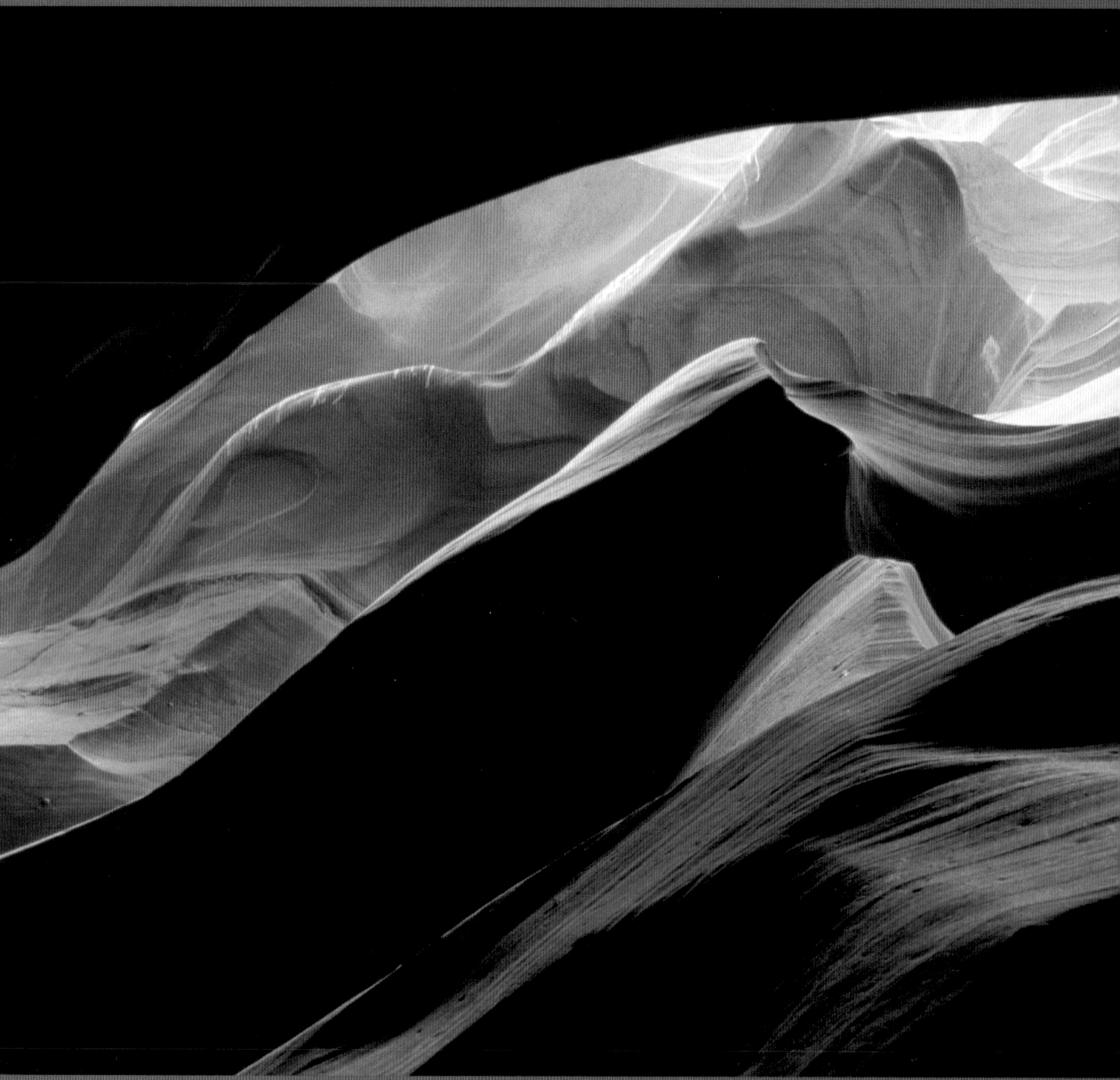

The Earth is like a blender in which rocks are moved around, broken, and crumbled. The fragments are deposited, forming different layers. Then weathering and erosion by wind and rain wear down and transform the rock. This produces mountains, cliffs, and sand dunes, among other features. The deposited material settles into layers of

MOUNTAINS OF SAND
Corkscrew Canyon in Arizona contains an array of shapes, colors, and textures. The sand varies from pink to yellow to red depending on the sunlight it receives.

TRAVERSING TIME 8-11

UNDER CONSTRUCTION 12-13

A CHANGING SURFACE 14-15

BEFORE ROCK, MINERAL 16-17

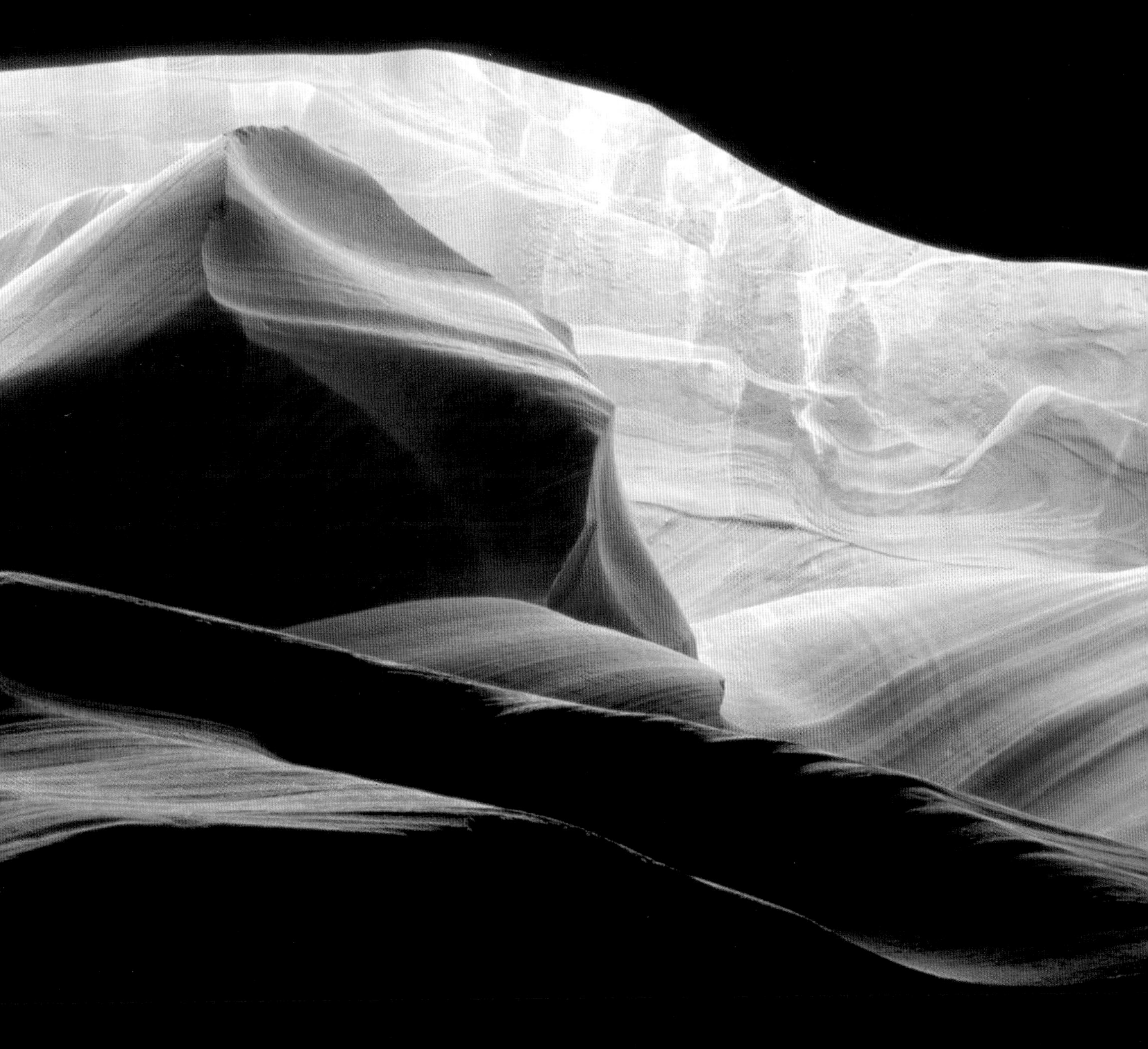

sediment that eventually become sedimentary rock. This rock cycle never stops. In 50 million years, no single mountain we know will exist in the same condition as it does today. ●

Traversing Time

Geologists and paleontologists use many sources to reconstruct the Earth's history. The analysis of rocks, minerals, and fossils found on the Earth's surface provides data about the deepest layers of the planet's crust and reveals both climatic and atmospheric changes that are often associated with catastrophes. Craters caused by the impact of meteorites and other bodies on the surface of the Earth also reveal valuable information about the history of the planet. ●

2 COLLISION AND FUSION
Heavy elements migrate.

Complex Structure

THE FORMATION OF THE INTERIOR
Cosmic materials began to accumulate, forming a growing celestial body, the precursor of the Earth. High temperatures combined with gravity caused the heaviest elements to migrate to the center of the planet and the lighter ones to move toward the surface. Under a rain of meteors, the external layers began to consolidate and form the Earth's crust. In the center, metals such as iron concentrated into a red-hot nucleus.

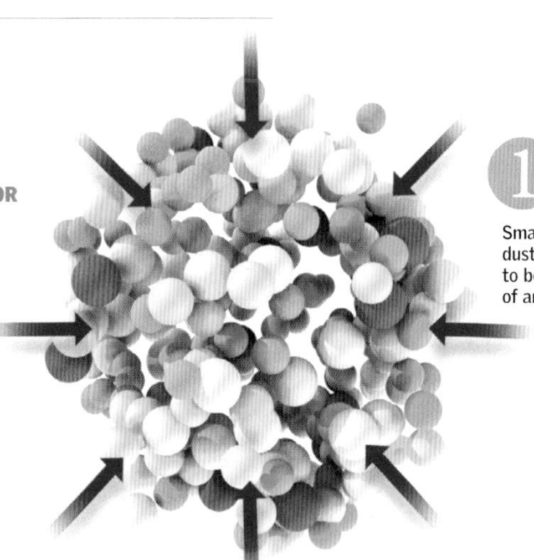

1 Small bodies and dust accumulate to become the size of an asteroid.

The oldest minerals, such as zircon, form.

The oldest rocks metamorphose, forming gneiss.

1,100
Rodinia, an early supercontinent, forms.

A meteorite falls in Sudbury, Ontario, Canada.

Age in millions of years

	4,600	2,500
ERA	Hadean	Proterozoic
PERIOD	Pregeologic	Precambrian
EPOCH		

Climate

Consolidation begins under a rain of meteors.

The Earth cools and the first ocean is formed.

ELEMENTS PRESENT ACCORDING TO THE TABLE
Existing in different combinations, the crust of the Earth contains the same elements today as those that were present when the planet was formed. The most abundant element in the crust is oxygen, which bonds with metals and nonmetals to form different compounds.

2,500
Glaciations: White Earth
The Earth undergoes the first of its massive global cooling events (glaciations).

800 Second glaciation
600 Last massive glaciation

Life

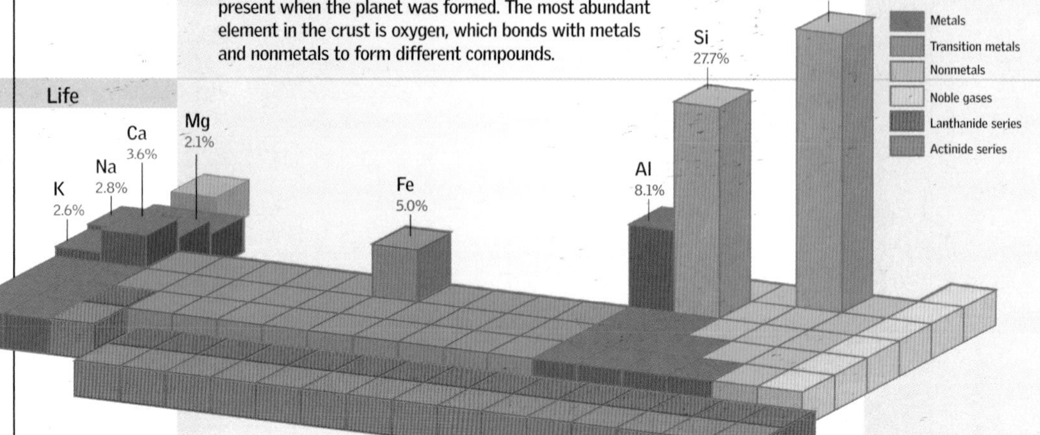

THE FIRST ANIMALS
Among the most mysterious fossils of the Precambrian Period are the remains of the Ediacaran fauna, the Earth's first-known animals. They lived at the bottom of the ocean. Many were round and reminiscent of jellyfish, while others were flat and sheetlike

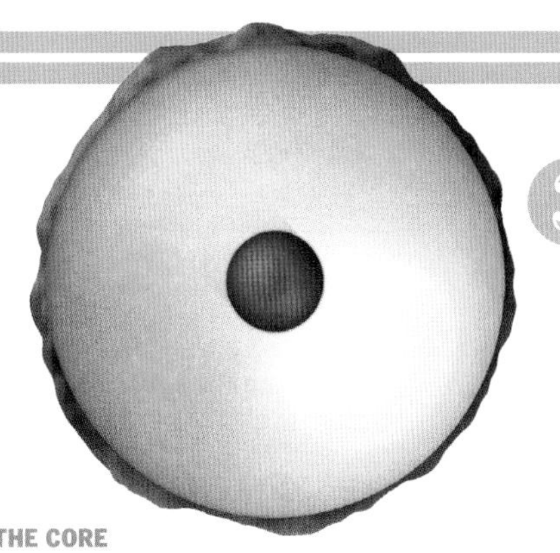

THE CORE
The Earth's core is extremely hot and is made mostly of iron and nickel.

3 METALLIC CORE
The light elements form the mantle.

Mountains

are external folds of the crust produced by extremely powerful forces occurring inside the Earth.

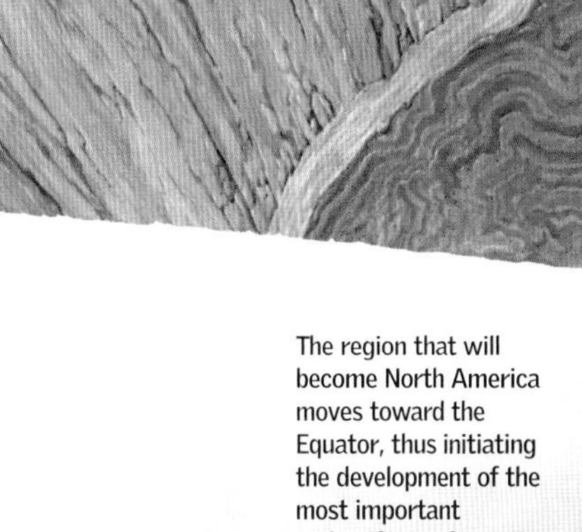

542
The supercontinent Panotia forms, containing portions of present-day continents. North America separates from Panotia.

OROGENIES
Geological history recognizes long periods (lasting millions of years) of intense mountain formation called orogenies. Each orogeny is characterized by its own particular materials and location.

The first major orogeny (Caledonian folding) begins. Gondwana moves toward the South Pole.

Laurentia and Baltica converge, creating the Caledonian range. Gneiss forms on the coast of Scotland.

The region that will become North America moves toward the Equator, thus initiating the development of the most important carboniferous formations. Gondwana moves slowly; the ocean floor spreads at a similar speed.

The fragments of continents combine to form a single continent called Pangea.

The Appalachian Mountains form. The formation of slate through sedimentation is at its peak.

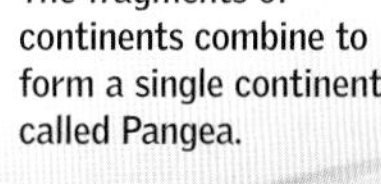

Baltica and Siberia clash, forming the Ural Mountains.

Eruptions of basalt occur in Siberia.

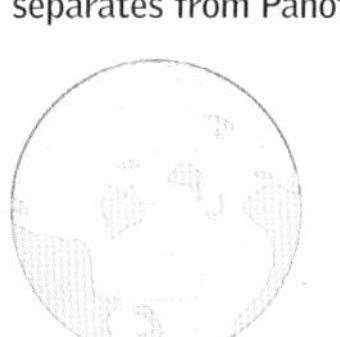

542	488.3	443.7	416	359.2	299

Paleozoic THE ERA OF PRIMITIVE LIFE

Cambrian	Ordovician	Silurian	Devonian	Carboniferous	Permian
Temperatures fall. The level of carbon dioxide (CO_2) in the atmosphere is 16 times higher than it is today.	It is thought that the Earth's atmosphere contained far less carbon dioxide during the Ordovician than today. Temperatures fluctuate within a range similar to what we experience today.	By this period, vertebrates with mandibles, such as the placoderms, osteichthyans (bony fish), and acanthodians, have already emerged.	Temperatures were typically warmer than today, and oxygen (O_2) levels attained their maximum.	Hot, humid climates produce exuberant forests in swamplands.	The largest carbon deposits we observe today form where forests previously existed.

THE CAMBRIAN EXPLOSION
Fossils from this time attest to the great diversity of marine animals and the emergence of different types of skeletal structures, such as those found in sponges and trilobites.

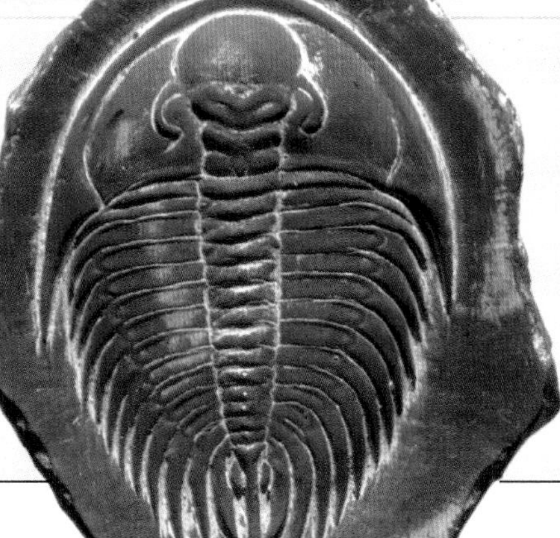

TRILOBITES
Marine arthropods with mineralized exoskeletons

SILURIAN
One of the first pisciform vertebrates, an armored fish without mandibles

The rocks of this period contain an abundance of fish fossils.

Areas of solid ground are populated by gigantic ferns.

Amphibians diversify and reptiles originate from one amphibian group to become the first amniotes. Winged insects such as dragonflies emerge.

Palm trees and conifers replace the vegetation from the Carboniferous Period.

MASS EXTINCTION
Near the end of the Permian Period, an estimated 95 percent of marine organisms and over two thirds of terrestrial ones perish in the greatest known mass extinction.

IMPACT FROM THE OUTSIDE

It is believed that a large meteor fell on Chicxulub, on the Yucatán Peninsula (Mexico), about 65 million years ago. The impact caused an explosion that created a cloud of ash mixed with carbon rocks. When the debris fell back to Earth, some experts believe it caused a great global fire.

The heat caused by the expansion of fragments from the impact together with the greenhouse effect brought about by the spreading of ashes in the stratosphere provoked a series of climatic changes. It is believed that this process resulted in the extinction of the dinosaurs.

62 miles (100 km)

The diameter of the crater produced by the impact of the meteor on the Yucatán Peninsula. It is now buried under almost 2 miles (3 km) of limestone.

Gondwana reappears.

Africa separates from South America, and the South Atlantic Ocean appears.

FORMATION OF MOUNTAIN CHAINS

60 Central Rocky Mountains

30 Alps

20 Himalayas

251	199.6	145.5	65.5	
Mesozoic THE ERA OF REPTILES			**Cenozoic** THE AGE OF MAMMALS	
Triassic	Jurassic	Cretaceous	Paleogene	
			Paleocene	Eocene

Triassic: Carbon dioxide levels increase. Average temperatures are higher than today.

Jurassic: The level of oxygen (O_2) in the atmosphere is much lower than today.

THE AGE OF FLOWERING PLANTS

At the end of the Cretaceous Period, the first angiosperms—plants with protected seeds, flowers, and fruits—appear.

The global average temperature is at least 62° F (17° C). The ice layer covering Antarctica late thickens.

Proliferation of insects

Appearance of dinosaurs

The first mammals evolve from a group of reptiles called Therapsida.

Birds emerge.

The dinosaurs undergo adaptive radiation.

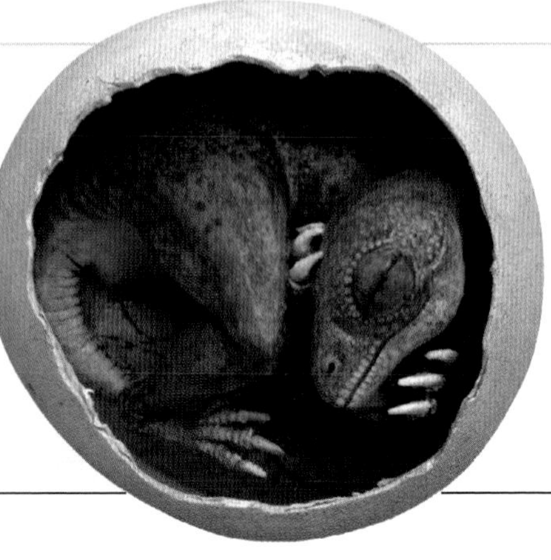

ALLOSAURUS
This carnivore measured 39 feet (12 m) long.

ANOTHER MASS EXTINCTION

Toward the end of the Cretaceous Period, about 50 percent of existing species disappear. The dinosaurs, the large marine reptiles (such as the Plesiosaurs), the flying creatures of that period (such as the Pterosaurs), and the ammonites (cephalopod mollusks) disappear from the Earth. At the beginning of the Cenozoic Era, most of the habitats of these extinct species begin to be occupied by mammals.

Elements in Equilibrium

Minerals, such as iron and silicates, are widely spread among the major constituents of the crust. Only the movements of the crust on the molten mantle disrupt their equilibrium.

North America and Europe drift apart. North and South America are joined at the end of this time period. The formation of Patagonia concludes, and an important overthrust raises the Andes mountain range.

The African Rift Zone and the Red Sea open up. The Indian protocontinent collides with Eurasia.

23.03

Neogene

Oligocene | Miocene | Pliocene | Pleistocene | Holocene

CRUST
The Earth's crust can reach a thickness of up to 6 miles (10 km) at the bottom of the ocean and up to 30 miles (50 km) on the continents.

LITHOSPHERE
The solid rock coating of the Earth, which includes the exterior of the mantle

MANTLE
The mantle is 1,800 miles (2,900 km) thick and is composed mainly of solid rock. Its temperature increases with depth. A notable component of the upper mantle is the asthenosphere, which is semisolid. In the asthenosphere, superficial rock layers that will eventually form the Earth's crust are melted.

CORE
Outer Core
The outer core is 1,400 miles (2,270 km) thick and contains melted iron, nickel, and other minor chemical compounds.

Inner Core
The inner core has a diameter of 756 miles (1,216 km). It is made of iron and nickel, which are solidified due to their exposure to high pressure and temperature conditions.

Temperatures drop to levels similar to those of today. The lower temperatures cause forests to shrink and grasslands to expand.

THE LAST GLACIATION

The most recent period of glaciation begins three million years ago and intensifies at the beginning of the Quaternary period. North Pole glaciers advance, and much of the Northern Hemisphere becomes covered in ice.

Vast development of feathered bird species and mammals covered with long fur

MAMMOTHS
Mammoths lived in Siberia. The cause of their extinction is still under debate.

HUMAN BEINGS APPEAR ON EARTH.

Although the oldest hominid fossils (Sahelanthropus) date back to seven million years ago, it is believed that modern humans emerged in Africa at the end of the Pleistocene. Humans migrated to Europe 100,000 years ago, although settling there was difficult because of the glacial climate. According to one hypothesis, our ancestors reached the American continent about 10,000 years ago by traveling across the area now known as the Bering Strait.

Under Construction

Our planet is not a dead body, complete and unchanging. It is an ever-changing system whose activity we experience all the time: volcanoes erupt, earthquakes occur, and new rocks emerge on the Earth's surface. All these phenomena, which originate in the interior of the planet, are studied in a branch of geology called internal geodynamics. This science analyzes processes, such as continental drift and isostatic movement, which originate with the movement of the crust and result in the raising and sinking of large areas. The movement of the Earth's crust also generates the conditions that form new rocks. This movement affects magmatism (the melting of materials that solidify to become igneous rocks) and metamorphism (the series of transformations occurring in solid materials that give rise to metamorphic rocks).

Magmatism

Magma is produced when the temperature in the mantle or crust reaches a level at which minerals with the lowest fusion point begin to melt. Because magma is less dense than the solid material surrounding it, it rises, and in so doing it cools and begins to crystallize. When this process occurs in the interior of the crust, plutonic or intrusive rocks, such as granite, are produced. If this process takes place on the outside, volcanic or effusive rocks, such as basalt, are formed.

Metamorphism

An increase in pressure and/or temperature causes rocks to become plastic and their minerals to become unstable. These rocks then chemically react with the substances surrounding them, creating different chemical combinations and thus causing new rocks to form. These rocks are called metamorphic rocks. Examples of this type of rock are marble, quartzite, and gneiss.

PRESSURE
This force gives rise to new metamorphic rocks, as older rocks fuse with the minerals that surround them.

TEMPERATURE
High temperatures make the rocks plastic and their minerals unstable.

Folding

Although solid, the materials forming the Earth's crust are elastic. The powerful forces of the Earth place stress upon the materials and create folds in the rock. When this happens, the ground rises and sinks. When this activity occurs on a large scale, it can create mountain ranges or chains. This activity typically occurs in the subduction zones.

Fracture

When the forces acting upon rocks become too intense, the rocks lose their plasticity and break, creating two types of fractures: joints and faults. When this process happens too abruptly, earthquakes occur. Joints are fissures and cracks, whereas faults are fractures in which blocks are displaced parallel to a fracture plane.

A Changing Surface

The molding of the Earth's crust is the product of two great destructive forces: weathering and erosion. Through the combination of these processes, rocks merge, disintegrate, and join again. Living organisms, especially plant roots and digging animals, cooperate with these geologic processes. Once the structure of the minerals that make up a rock is disrupted, the minerals disintegrate and fall to the mercy of the rain and wind, which erode them.

Erosion

External agents, such as water, wind, air, and living beings, either acting separately or together, wear down, and their loose fragments may be transported. This process is known as erosion. In dry regions, the wind transports grains of sand that strike and polish exposed rocks. On the coast, wave action slowly eats away at the rocks.

EOLIAN PROCESSES
The wind drags small particles against the rocks. This wears them down and produces new deposits of either loess or sand depending on the size of the particle.

HYDROLOGIC PROCESSES
All types of moving water slowly wear down rock surfaces and carry loose particles away. The size of the particles that are carried away from the rock surface depends on the volume and speed of the flowing water. High-volume and high-velocity water can move larger particles.

Weathering

Mechanical agents can disintegrate rocks, and chemical agents can decompose them. Disintegration and decomposition can result from the actions of plant roots, heat, cold, wind, and acid rain. The breaking down of rock is a slow but inexorable process.

CHEMICAL PROCESSES

The mineral components of rocks are altered. They either become new minerals or are released in solution.

MECHANICAL PROCESSES

A variety of forces can cause rock fragments to break into smaller pieces, either by acting on the rocks directly or by transporting rock fragments that chip away at the rock surface.

TEMPERATURE

When the temperature of the air changes significantly over a few hours, it causes rocks to expand and contract abruptly. The daily repetition of this phenomenon can cause rocks to rupture.

WATER

In a liquid or frozen state, water penetrates into the rock fissures, causing them to expand and shatter.

Transportation and Sedimentation

In this process, materials eroded by the wind or water are carried away and deposited at lower elevations, and these new deposits can later turn into other rocks.

Before Rock, Mineral

The planet on which we live can be seen as a large rock or, more precisely, as a large sphere composed of many types of rocks. These rocks are composed of tiny fragments of one or more materials. These materials are minerals, which result from the interaction of different chemical elements, each of which is stable only under specific conditions of pressure and temperature. Both rocks and minerals are studied in the branches of geology called petrology and mineralogy.

12 million years ago

rock batholiths formed during a period of great volcanic activity and created the Torres del Paine and its high mountains.

TORRES DEL PAINE
Chilean Patagonia

Latitude 52° 20´ S
Longitude 71° 55´ W

Composition	Granite
Highest summit	Paine Grande (10,000 feet [3,050 m])
Surface	598 acres (242 ha)

Torres del Paine National Park is located in Chile between the massif of the Andes and the Patagonian steppes.

From Minerals to Rocks

From a chemical perspective, a mineral is a homogeneous substance. A rock, on the other hand, is composed of different chemical substances, which, in turn, are components of minerals. The mineral components of rocks are also those of mountains. Thus, according to this perspective, it is possible to distinguish between rocks and minerals.

QUARTZ
Composed of silica, quartz gives rock a white color.

MICA
Composed of thin, shiny sheets of silicon, aluminum, potassium, and other minerals, mica can be black or colorless.

GRANITE
Rock composed of feldspar, quartz, and mica

FELDSPAR
A light-colored silicate, feldspar makes up a large part of the crust.

CHANGE OF STATE

Temperature and pressure play a prominent part in rock transformation. Inside the Earth, liquid magma is produced. When it reaches the surface, it solidifies. A similar process happens to water when it freezes upon reaching 32° F (0° C).

Minerals

Dallol is basically a desert of minerals whose ivory-colored crust is scattered with green ponds and towers of sulfur salts in shades of orange. Some minerals belong to a very special class. Known as gems, they are sought and hoarded for their great beauty. The most valuable gems are diamonds.

DALLOL VOLCANO
Located in Ethiopia, Dallol is the only non-oceanic volcano on Earth below sea level, making it one of the hottest places on the planet. Sulfur and other minerals that spring from this volcano create very vivid colors.

YOU ARE WHAT YOU HAVE 20-21
A QUESTION OF STYLE 22-23
HOW TO RECOGNIZE MINERALS 24-25
A DESERT OF MINERALS 26-27
THE ESSENCE OF CRYSTALS 28-29
CRYSTALLINE SYMMETRY 30-31
PRECIOUS CRYSTALS 32-33
DIAMONDS IN HISTORY 34-35
THE MOST COMMON MINERALS 36-37
THE NONSILICATES 38-39

Did you know it took human beings thousands of years to separate metal from rock? Did you also know that certain nonmetallic minerals are valued for their usefulness? Graphite, for instance, is used to make pencils; gypsum is used in construction; and halite, also known as salt, is used in cooking. ●

You Are What You Have

Minerals are the "bricks" of materials that make up the Earth and all other solid bodies in the universe. They are usually defined both by their chemical composition and by their orderly internal structure. Most are solid crystalline substances. However, some minerals have a disordered internal structure and are simply amorphous solids similar to glass. Studying minerals helps us to understand the origin of the Earth. Minerals are classified according to their composition and internal structure, as well as by the properties of hardness, weight, color, luster, and transparency. Although more than 4,000 minerals have been discovered, only about 30 are common on the Earth's surface.

Components

The basic components of minerals are the chemical elements listed on the periodic table. Minerals are classified as native if they are found in isolation, contain only one element, and occur in their purest state. On the other hand, they are classified as compound if they are composed of two or more elements. Most minerals fall into the compound category.

MINERALS COME FROM

112 elements

listed in the periodic table.

1 NATIVE MINERALS

These minerals are classified into:

A- METALS AND INTERMETALS
Native minerals have high thermal and electrical conductivity, a typically metallic luster, low hardness, ductility, and malleability. They are easy to identify and include gold, copper, and lead.

GOLD
An excellent thermal and electrical conductor. Acids have little or no effect on it.

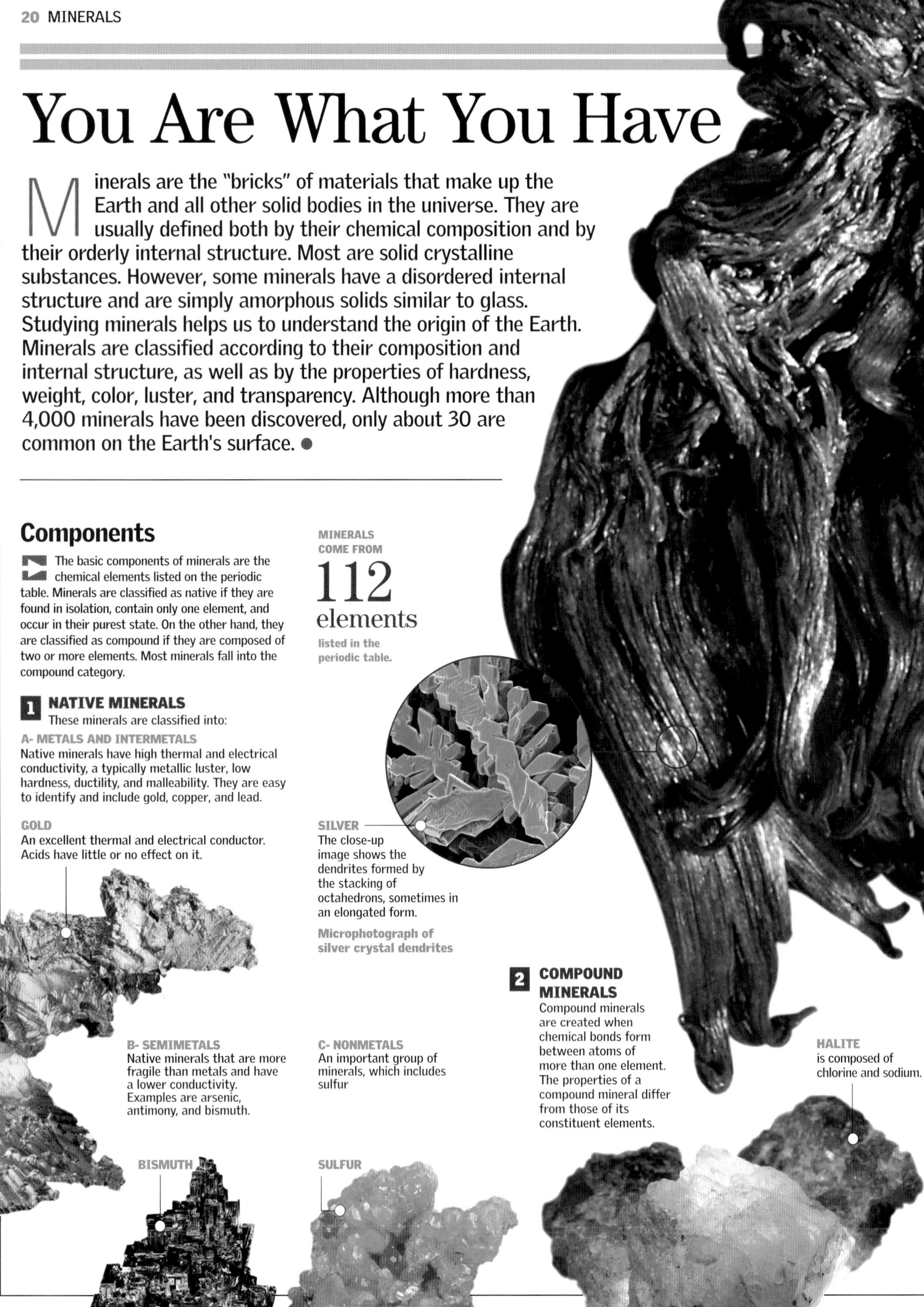

SILVER
The close-up image shows the dendrites formed by the stacking of octahedrons, sometimes in an elongated form.

Microphotograph of silver crystal dendrites

B- SEMIMETALS
Native minerals that are more fragile than metals and have a lower conductivity. Examples are arsenic, antimony, and bismuth.

BISMUTH

C- NONMETALS
An important group of minerals, which includes sulfur

SULFUR

2 COMPOUND MINERALS

Compound minerals are created when chemical bonds form between atoms of more than one element. The properties of a compound mineral differ from those of its constituent elements.

HALITE
is composed of chlorine and sodium.

Polymorphism

A phenomenon in which the same chemical composition can create multiple structures and, consequently, result in the creation of several different minerals. The transition of one polymorphous variant into another, facilitated by temperature or pressure conditions, can be fast or slow and either reversible or irreversible.

Chemical Composition	Crystallization System	Mineral
$CaCO_3$	Trigonal	**Calcite**
$CaCO_3$	Rhombic	**Aragonite**
FeS_2	Cubic	**Pyrite**
FeS_2	Rhombic	**Marcasite**
C	Cubic	Diamond
C	Hexagonal	Graphite

MORE THAN
4,000 types of minerals
have been recognized by the International Association of Mineralogy.

DIAMOND AND GRAPHITE
A mineral's internal structure influences its hardness. Both graphite and diamond are composed only of carbon; however, they have different degrees of hardness.

Diamond

Graphite

Carbon Atom

Model demonstrating how one atom bonds to the other four

Each atom is joined to four other atoms of the same type. The carbon network extends in three dimensions by means of strong covalent bonds. This provides the mineral with an almost unbreakable hardness.

Hardness of 10
on the Mohs scale

Atoms form hexagons that are strongly interconnected in parallel sheets. This structure allows the sheets to slide over one another.

Hardness of 1
on the Mohs scale

Isotypic Minerals

Isomorphism happens when minerals with the same structure, such as halite and galena, exchange cations. The structure remains the same, but the resulting substance is different, because one ion has been exchanged for another. An example of this process is siderite (rhombic $FeCO_3$), which gradually changes to magnesite ($MgCO_3$) when it trades its iron (Fe) for similarly-sized magnesium (Mg). Because the ions are the same size, the structure remains unchanged.

HALITE AND GALENA

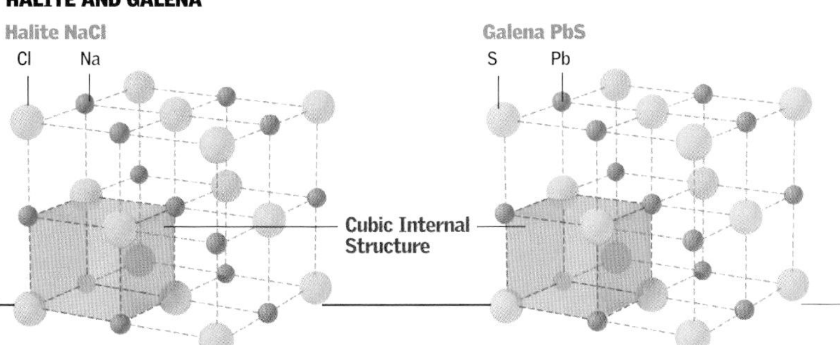

A Question of Style

Optical properties involve a mineral's response to the presence of light. This characteristic can be analyzed under a petrographic microscope, which differs from ordinary microscopes in that it has two devices that polarize light. This feature makes it possible to determine some of the optical responses of the mineral. However, the most precise way to identify a mineral by its optical properties is to use an X-ray diffractometer. ●

Color

is one of the most striking properties of minerals. However, in determining the identity of a mineral, color is not always useful. Some minerals never change color; they are called idiochromatic. Others whose colors are variable are called allochromatic. A mineral's color changes can be related, among other things, to the presence of impurities or inclusions (solid bodies) inside of it.

INHERENT COLOR

Some minerals always have the same color; one example is malachite.

MALACHITE

SULFUR

EXOTIC COLOR

A mineral can have several shades, depending on its impurities or inclusions.

QUARTZ

ROCK CRYSTAL
Colorless; the purest state of quartz

Other secondary minerals, known as exotic minerals, are responsible for giving quartz its color; when it lacks exotic minerals, quartz is colorless.

ROSE
The presence of manganese results in a pink color.

CITRINE
The presence of iron produces a very pale yellow color.

SMOKY
Dark, brown, or gray minerals

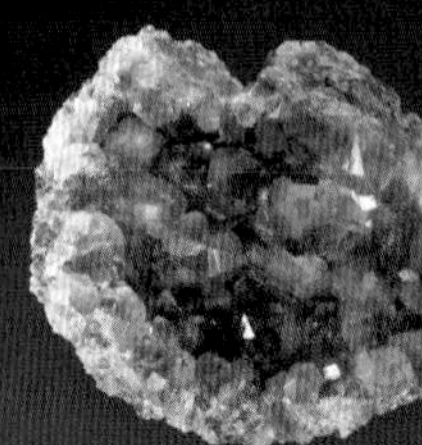

AMETHYST
The presence of iron in a ferric state results in a purple color.

COLOR STREAK

More reliable than a mineral's color is its streak (the color of the fine powder left when the mineral is rubbed across a hard white surface).

HEMATITE
Color: Black

Streak Color:
Reddish Brown

AGATE
A type of chalcedony, a cryptocrystalline variety of quartz, of nonuniform coloring

Agates crystallize in banded patterns because of the environments in which they form. They fill the cavities of rocks by precipitating out of aqueous solutions at low temperatures. Their colors reflect the porosity of the stone, its degree of inclusions, and the crystallization process.

Luminescence

Certain minerals emit light when they are exposed to particular sources of energy. A mineral is fluorescent if it lights up when exposed to ultraviolet rays or X-rays. It is phosphorescent if it keeps glowing after the energy source is removed. Some minerals will also respond to cathode rays, ordinary light, heat, or other electric currents.

METALLIC
Minerals in this class are completely opaque, a characteristic typical of native elements, such as copper, and sulfides, such as galena.

Refraction and Luster

Refraction is related to the speed with which light moves through a crystal. Depending on how light propagates through them, minerals can be classified as monorefringent or birefringent. Luster results from reflection and refraction of light on the surface of a mineral. In general, it depends on the index of refraction of a mineral's surface, the absorption of incident light, and other factors, such as concrete characteristics of the observed surface (for instance, degree of smoothness and polish). Based on their luster, minerals can be divided into three categories.

SUBMETALLIC
Minerals in this class have a luster that is neither metallic nor nonmetallic.

NONMETALLIC
Minerals in this class transmit light when cut into very thin sheets. They can have several types of luster: vitreous (quartz), pearlescent, silky (talc), resinous, or earthy.

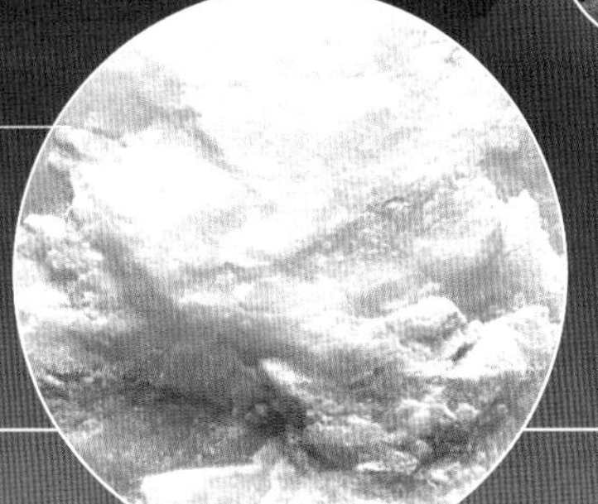

Streak

is the color of a mineral's fine powder, which can be used to identify it.

How to Recognize Minerals

A mineral's physical properties are very important for recognizing it at first glance. One physical property is hardness. One mineral is harder than another when the former can scratch the latter. A mineral's degree of hardness is based on a scale, ranging from 1 to 10, that was created by German mineralogist Friedrich Mohs. Another physical property of a mineral is its tenacity, or cohesion—that is, its degree of resistance to rupture, deformation, or crushing. Yet another is magnetism, the ability of a mineral to be attracted by a magnet.

Exfoliation and Fracture

When a mineral tends to break along the planes of weak bonds in its crystalline structure, it separates into flat sheets parallel to its surface. This is called exfoliation. Minerals that do not exfoliate when they break are said to exhibit fracture, which typically occurs in irregular patterns.

TYPES OF EXFOLIATION

Cubic

Octahedral

Dodecahedral

Rhombohedral

Prismatic and Pinacoidal

Pinacoidal (Basal)

TOURMALINE is a mineral of the silicate group.

COLOR Some tourmaline crystals can have two or more colors.

FRACTURE can be irregular, conchoidal, smooth, splintery, or earthy.

An uneven, splintery mineral surface

MOHS SCALE ranks 10 minerals, from the softest to the hardest. Each mineral can be scratched by the one that ranks above it.

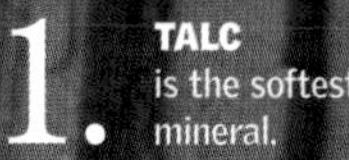
1. **TALC** is the softest mineral.

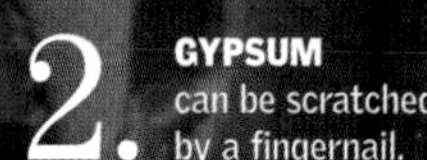
2. **GYPSUM** can be scratched by a fingernail.

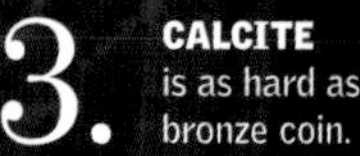
3. **CALCITE** is as hard as a bronze coin.

4. **FLUORITE** can be scratched by a knife.

5. **APATITE** can be scratche[d] by a piece of g[lass]

Electricity Generation

Piezoelectricity and pyroelectricity are phenomena exhibited by certain crystals, such as quartz, which acquire a polarized charge because exposure to temperature change or mechanical tension creates a difference in electrical potential at their ends.

PIEZOELECTRICITY
The generation of electric currents that can occur when mechanical tension redistributes the negative and positive charges in a crystal. Tourmaline is an example.

PYROELECTRICITY
The generation of electric currents that can occur when a crystal is subjected to changes in temperature and, consequently, changes in volume.

HEAT
Positive charge
Negative charge

DENSITY
reflects the structure and chemical composition of a mineral. Gold and platinum are among the most dense minerals.

7 to 7.5
IS THE HARDNESS OF THE TOURMALINE ON THE MOHS SCALE.

6. **ORTHOCLASE** can be scratched by a drill bit.

7. **QUARTZ** can be scratched by tempered steel.

8. **TOPAZ** can be scratched with a steel file.

9. **CORUNDUM** can be scratched only by diamond.

10. **DIAMOND** is the hardest mineral.

A Desert of Minerals

The Dallol region is part of the Afar depression in Ethiopia. It is known as "the devil's kitchen" because it has the highest average temperature in the world, 93° F (34° C). Dallol is basically a desert of minerals with an ivory-colored crust, sprinkled with green ponds and towers of sulfurous salt, in shades of orange, called hornitos (8 to 10 feet [2.5–3 m] high), many of which are active and spit out boiling water.

OLD, INACTIVE HORNITO

ETHIOPIA
Latitude 9° N
Longitude 39° E

DALLOL VOLCANO

Location	Afar Depression
Type of volcano	Explosion Crater
Elevation	–125 feet (–48 m)
Last eruption	1926
Annual salt extraction	135,000 tons

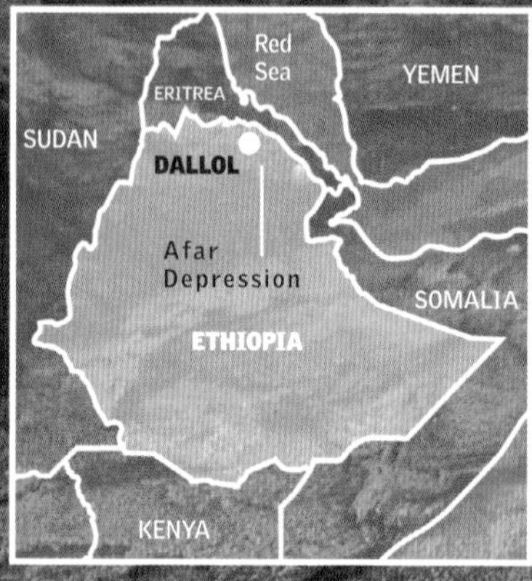

CROSS SECTION

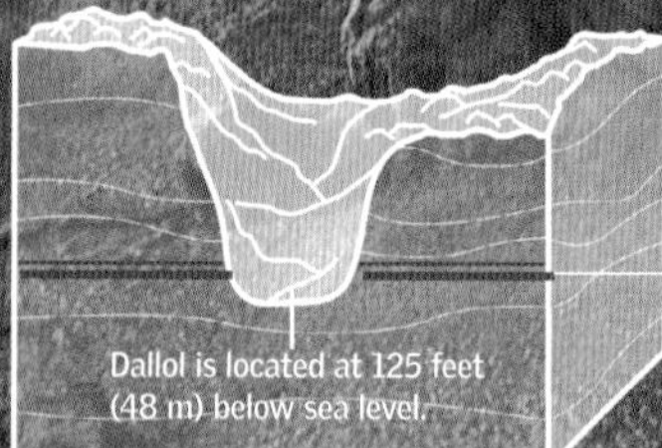

3.3 billion tons
(3 billion metric tons)

TOTAL RESERVE OF ROCK SALT IN THE AFAR DEPRESSION

MINERALIZATION PROCESS

Water expelled from its magmatic spring erupts, surfacing as thermal water. When the water evaporates, salt deposits are formed.

3 HEAT The heat causes the water to evaporate. Salt deposits form on the surface.

2 ASCENT Water rises to the surface through layers of salt and sulfur deposits.

1 HEAT Volcanic heat warms the water underground.

YOUNG DEPOSIT Newer deposits have a white color, which becomes darker over time.

POND Boiling water emerges from the hornitos and forms small ponds on the surface.

OLD DEPOSIT The dark coloring indicates that this depos is several months old.

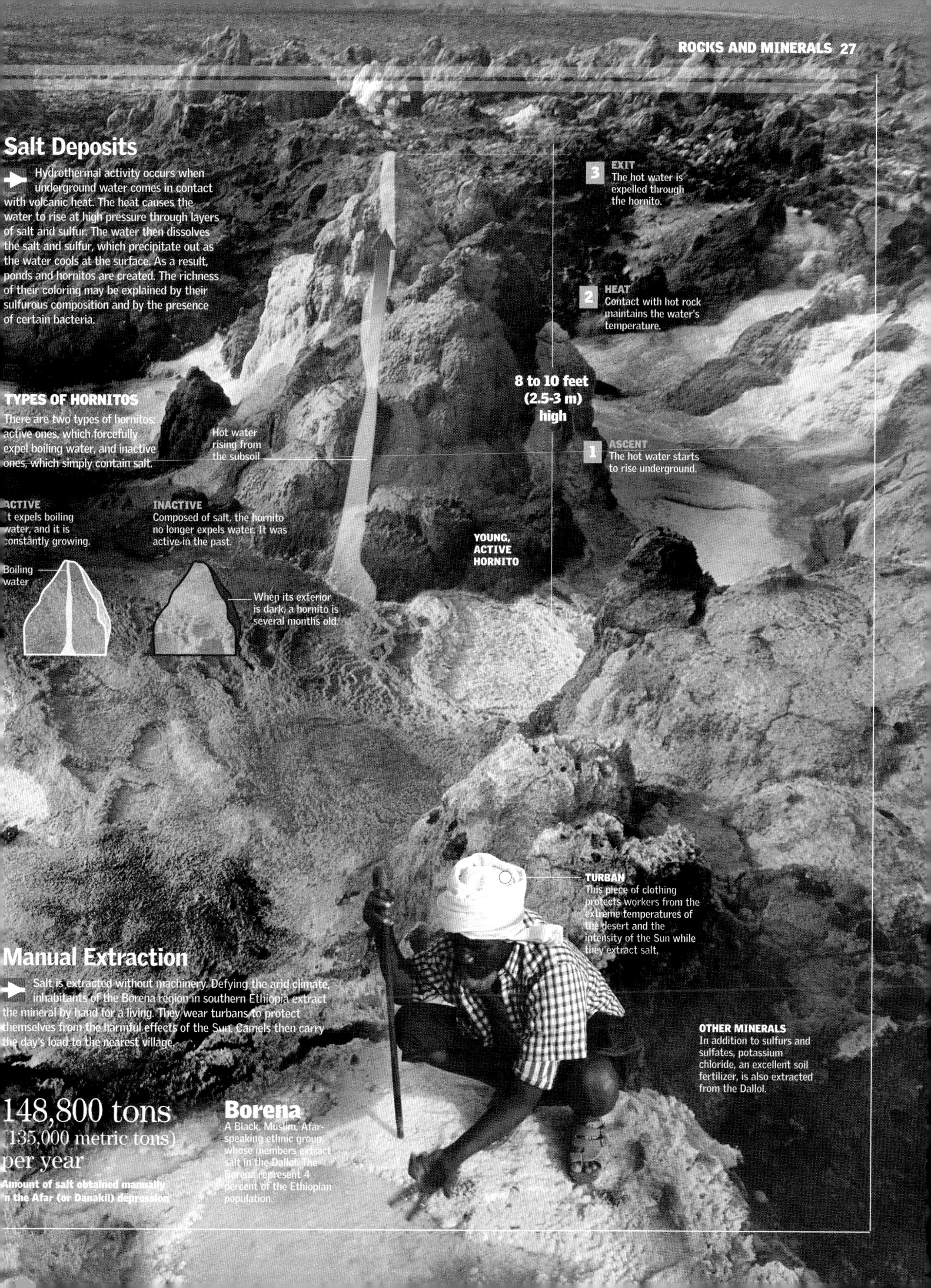

Salt Deposits

Hydrothermal activity occurs when underground water comes in contact with volcanic heat. The heat causes the water to rise at high pressure through layers of salt and sulfur. The water then dissolves the salt and sulfur, which precipitate out as the water cools at the surface. As a result, ponds and hornitos are created. The richness of their coloring may be explained by their sulfurous composition and by the presence of certain bacteria.

3 EXIT The hot water is expelled through the hornito.

2 HEAT Contact with hot rock maintains the water's temperature.

8 to 10 feet (2.5-3 m) high

1 ASCENT The hot water starts to rise underground.

Hot water rising from the subsoil

YOUNG, ACTIVE HORNITO

TYPES OF HORNITOS

There are two types of hornitos: active ones, which forcefully expel boiling water, and inactive ones, which simply contain salt.

ACTIVE
It expels boiling water, and it is constantly growing.

Boiling water

INACTIVE
Composed of salt, the hornito no longer expels water. It was active in the past.

When its exterior is dark, a hornito is several months old.

TURBAN
This piece of clothing protects workers from the extreme temperatures of the desert and the intensity of the Sun while they extract salt.

Manual Extraction

Salt is extracted without machinery. Defying the arid climate, inhabitants of the Borena region in southern Ethiopia extract the mineral by hand for a living. They wear turbans to protect themselves from the harmful effects of the Sun. Camels then carry the day's load to the nearest village.

OTHER MINERALS
In addition to sulfurs and sulfates, potassium chloride, an excellent soil fertilizer, is also extracted from the Dallol.

148,800 tons
(135,000 metric tons)
per year

Amount of salt obtained manually in the Afar (or Danakil) depression

Borena
A Black, Muslim, Afar-speaking ethnic group, whose members extract salt in the Dallol. The Borena represent 4 percent of the Ethiopian population.

The Essence of Crystals

All minerals take on a crystalline structure as they form. Most crystals originate when molten rock from inside the Earth cools and hardens. Crystallography is the branch of science that studies the growth, shape, and geometric characteristics of crystals. The arrangement of atoms in a crystal can be determined using X-ray diffraction. The relationship between chemical composition of the crystal, arrangement of atoms, and bond strengths among atoms is studied in crystallographic chemistry.

IONIC BOND

Typical of metallic elements that tend to lose electrons in the presence of other atoms with a negative charge. When a chlorine atom captures an electron from a sodium atom (metallic), both become electrically charged and mutually attract each other. The sodium atom shares an electron (negative charge) and becomes positively charged, whereas the chlorine completes its outer shell, becoming negative.

BEFORE BONDING	AFTER BONDING
Na	Na+
Cl	Cl-

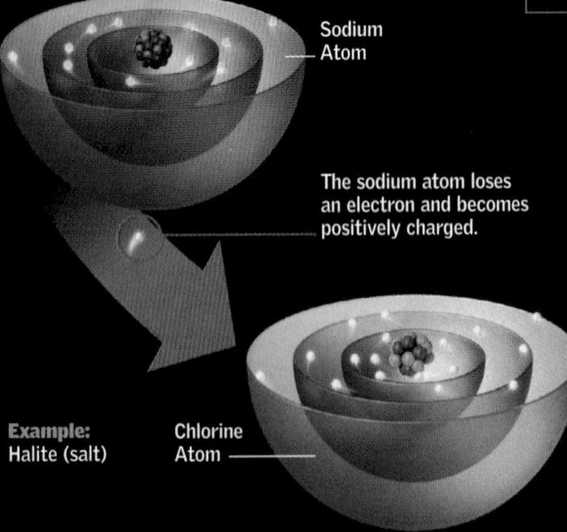

Example:
Halite (salt)

The chlorine atom gains an electron (negative charge) and becomes a negatively charged ion (anion).

Sodium Atom

The anion and the cation (positive ion) are electrically attracted to one another. They bond, forming a new, stable compound.

COVALENT BOND

This type of bond occurs between two nonmetallic elements, such as nitrogen and oxygen. The atoms are geometrically organized to share electrons from their outer shells. This way, the whole structure becomes more stable.

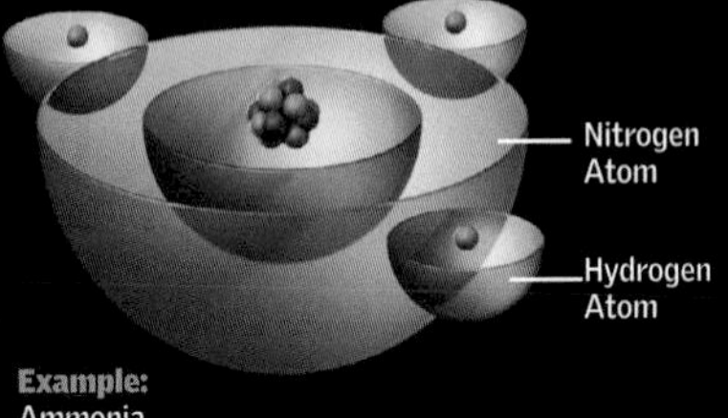

Example:
Ammonia

The nitrogen atom needs three electrons to stabilize its outer shell; the hydrogen atom needs only one. The union of all four atoms creates a stable state.así la logran.

CRYSTALS OF COMMON SALT
When salt forms larger crystals, their shape can be seen under a microscope.

INTERNAL CRYSTALLINE NETWORK

A crystal's structure is repeated on the inside, even in the arrangement of its smallest parts: chlorine and sodium ions. In this case, the electrical forces (attraction among opposite ions and repulsion among similar ones) form cubes, which creates stability. However, different mineral compositions can take many other possible forms.

LEGEND

Chlorine Anion
This nonmetal can only acquire a maximum negative charge of 1.

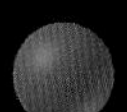

Sodium Cation
This metal can only acquire a maximum positive charge of 1.

7 Crystalline Systems

The combination of two ions results in a cubic form. When there are more than two ions, other structures are formed.

BASIC FORMS OF ATOMIC BONDING

This graphic represents an atom's internal crystalline network.

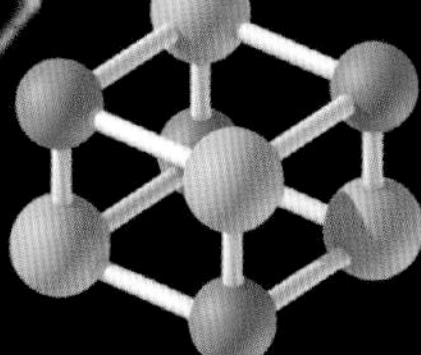

CUBE
Salt (Halite)
1 chlorine atom +
1 sodium atom

TETRAHEDRON
Silica
1 silicon atom +
4 oxygen atoms

DIFFERENCES BETWEEN CRYSTAL AND GLASS

Glass is an amorphous solid. Because it solidifies quickly, the particles lose mobility before organizing themselves.

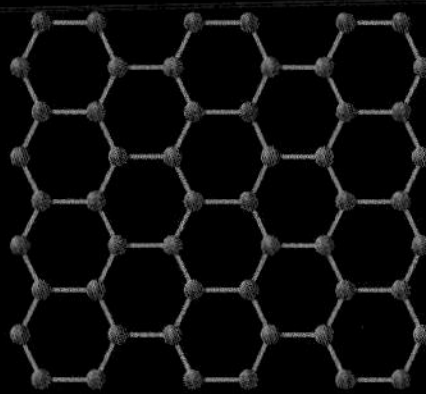

ATOMIC MODEL OF A CRYSTAL
The particles combine slowly in regular, stable shapes.

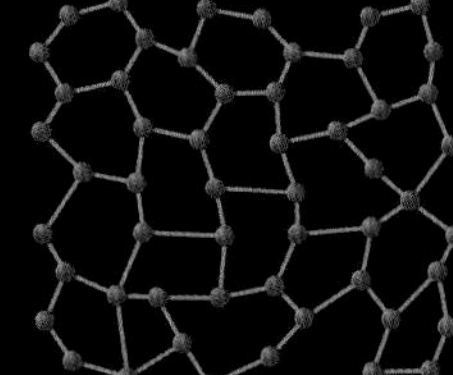

ATOMIC MODEL OF GLASS
Solidification prevents the particles from organizing themselves. This makes the structure irregular.

CUBIC STRUCTURE
is created through the spatial equilibrium between different ions, which attract each other, and similar ions, which repel each other.

Crystalline Symmetry

There are more than 4,000 minerals on Earth. They appear in nature in two ways: without an identifiable form or with a definite arrangement of atoms. The external expressions of these arrangements are called crystals, of which there are 32 classes. Crystals are characterized by their organized atomic structure, called a crystalline network, built from a fundamental unit (unit cell). These networks can be categorized into the seven crystalline systems according to the crystal's arrangement. They can also be organized into 14 three-dimensional networks, known as the Bravais lattices.

Typical Characteristics

A crystal is a homogeneous solid whose chemical elements exhibit an organized internal structure. A unit cell refers to the distribution of atoms or molecules whose repetition in three dimensions makes up the crystalline structure. The existence of elements with shared symmetry allows the 32 crystal classes to be categorized into seven groups. These groups are based on pure geometric shapes, such as cubes, prisms, and pyramids.

LEGEND

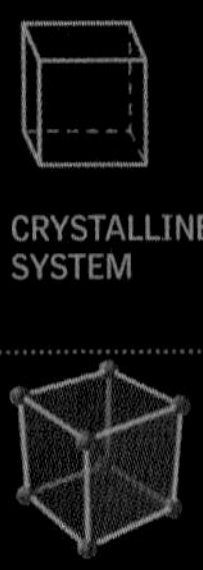

CRYSTALLINE SYSTEM

BRAVAIS LATTICES

THE MOST COMMON SHAPES

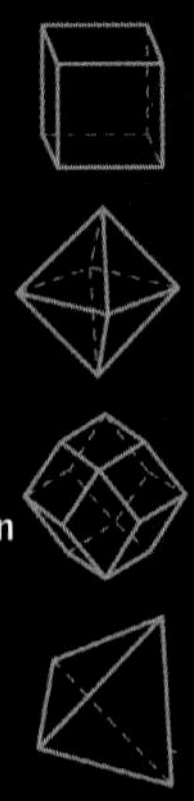

Cube

Octahedron

Rhombo-dodecahedron

Tetrahedron

Cubic

Three crystallographic axes meet at 90° angles.

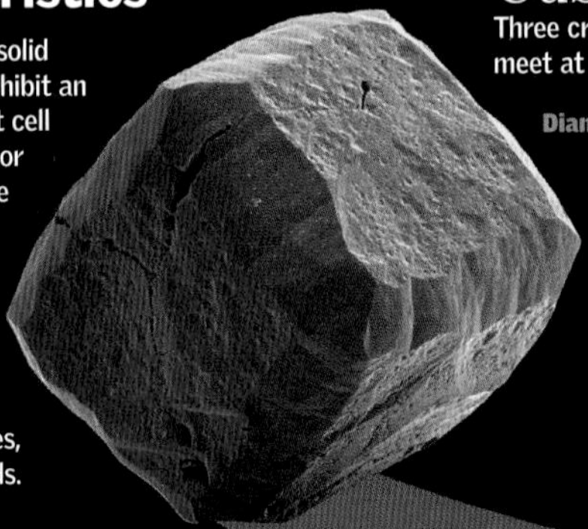

Diamond

Hexagonal

prisms have six sides, with 120º angles. From one end, the cross section is hexagonal.

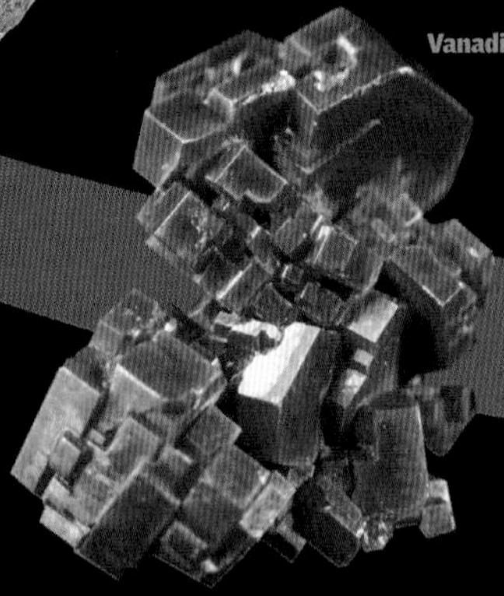

Vanadinite

Hexagonal Prism

Hexagonal Bipyramid

Hexagonal Prism Combined with Hexagonal Bipyramid

Hexagonal Prism Combined with Basal Pinacoid

Monoclinic

Prisms look like tetragonal crystals cut at an angle. Their axes do not meet at 90º angles.

Brazilianite

Prisms Combined with Pinacoids

Prism

Simple Monoclinic Network

Monoclinic Network Centered on its Bases

Bravais Lattices

In 1850, Auguste Bravais demonstrated theoretically that atoms can be organized into only 14 types of three-dimensional networks. These network types are therefore named after him.

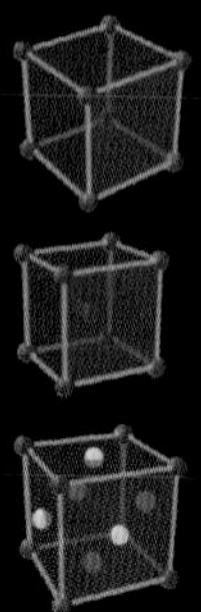

Simple Cubic Network

Body-centered Cubic Network

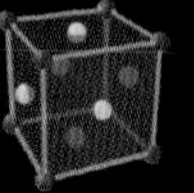

Face-centered Cubic Network

Only 14 network combinations are possible.

THESE COMBINATIONS ARE CALLED BRAVAIS LATTICES.

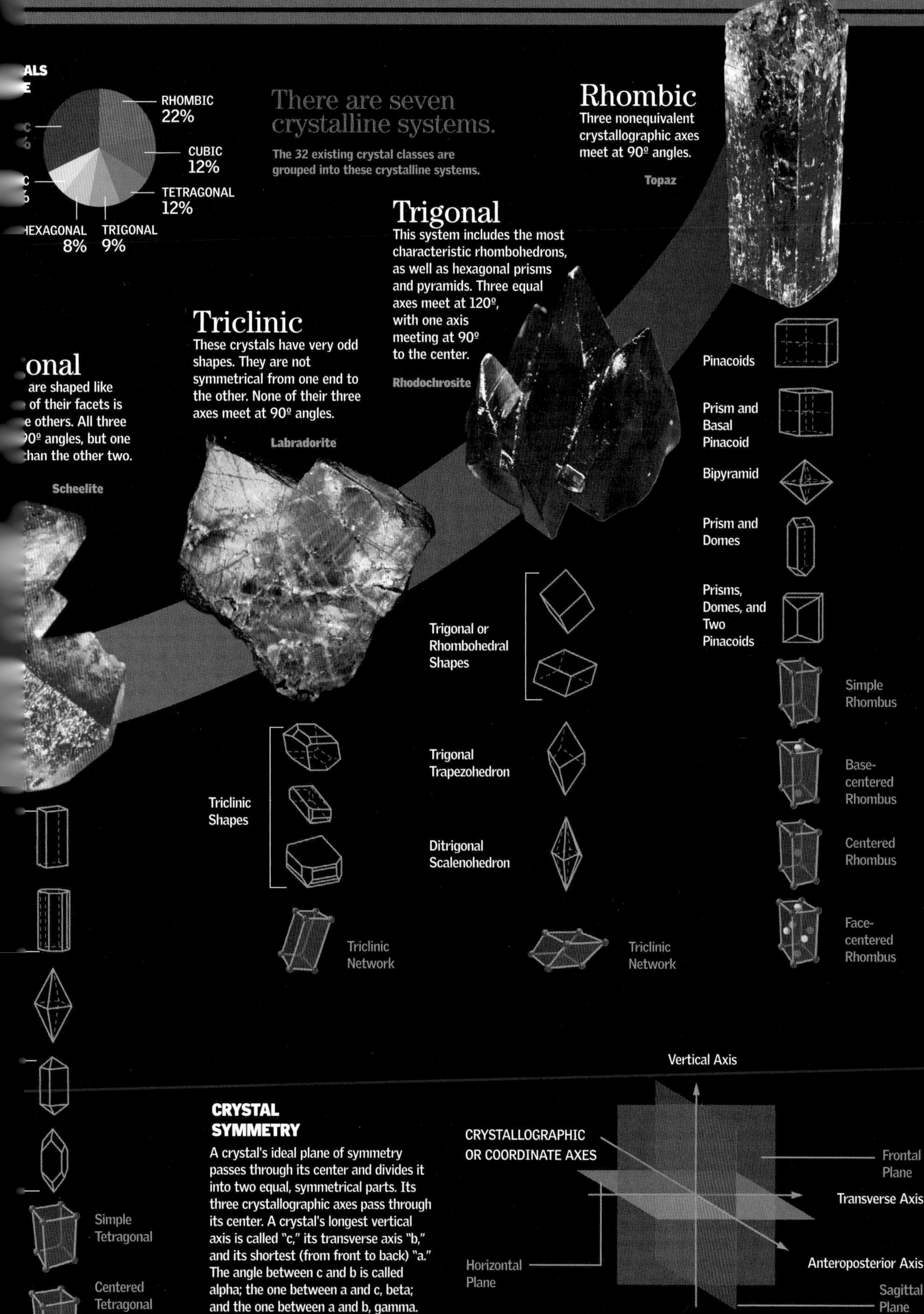

RHOMBIC 22%
CUBIC 12%
TETRAGONAL 12%
HEXAGONAL 8%
TRIGONAL 9%
There are seven crystalline systems.
The 32 existing crystal classes are grouped into these crystalline systems.
Rhombic
Three nonequivalent crystallographic axes meet at 90º angles.
Topaz
Trigonal
This system includes the most characteristic rhombohedrons, as well as hexagonal prisms and pyramids. Three equal axes meet at 120º, with one axis meeting at 90º to the center.
Rhodochrosite
Triclinic
These crystals have very odd shapes. They are not symmetrical from one end to the other. None of their three axes meet at 90º angles.
Labradorite
onal
are shaped like
of their facets is
e others. All three
0º angles, but one
han the other two.
Scheelite
Pinacoids
Prism and Basal Pinacoid
Bipyramid
Prism and Domes
Prisms, Domes, and Two Pinacoids
Simple Rhombus
Base-centered Rhombus
Centered Rhombus
Face-centered Rhombus
Trigonal or Rhombohedral Shapes
Trigonal Trapezohedron
Ditrigonal Scalenohedron
Triclinic Network
Triclinic Shapes
Triclinic Network
Simple Tetragonal
Centered Tetragonal
CRYSTAL SYMMETRY
A crystal's ideal plane of symmetry passes through its center and divides it into two equal, symmetrical parts. Its three crystallographic axes pass through its center. A crystal's longest vertical axis is called "c," its transverse axis "b," and its shortest (from front to back) "a." The angle between c and b is called alpha; the one between a and c, beta; and the one between a and b, gamma.
Vertical Axis
CRYSTALLOGRAPHIC OR COORDINATE AXES
Frontal Plane
Transverse Axis
Horizontal Plane
Anteroposterior Axis
Sagittal Plane

Precious Crystals

Precious stones are characterized by their beauty, color, transparency, and rarity. Examples are diamonds, emeralds, rubies, and sapphires. Compared to other gems, semiprecious stones are composed of minerals of lesser value. Today diamonds are the most prized gem for their "fire," luster and extreme hardness. The origin of diamonds goes back millions of years, but people began to cut them only in the 14th century. Most diamond deposits are located in South Africa, Namibia, and Australia.

Diamond

Mineral composed of crystallized carbon in a cubic system. The beauty of its glow is due to a very high refraction index and the great dispersion of light in its interior, which creates an array of colors. It is the hardest of all minerals, and it originates underground at great depths.

1 EXTRACTION

Diamonds are obtained from kimberlite pipes left over from old volcanic eruptions, which brought the diamonds up from great depths.

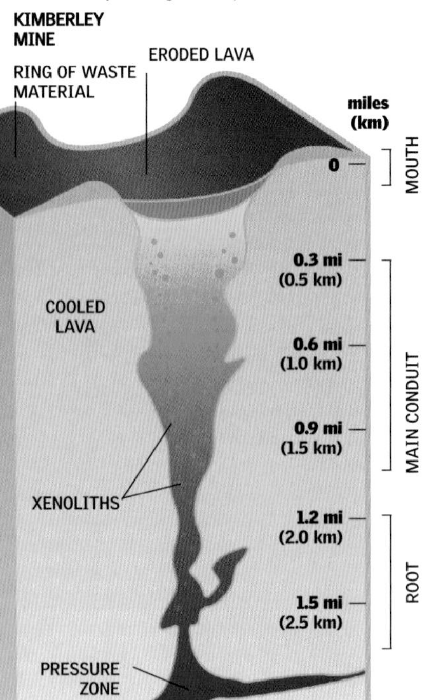

2 CUTTING AND CARVING

The diamond will be cut by another diamond to reach final perfection. This task is carried out by expert cutters.

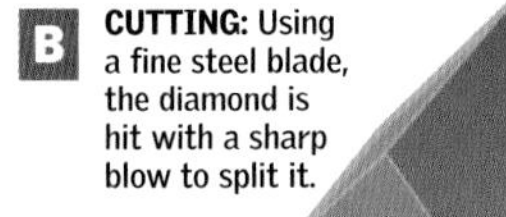

C CARVING: With a chisel, hammer, and circular saws, the diamond is shaped.

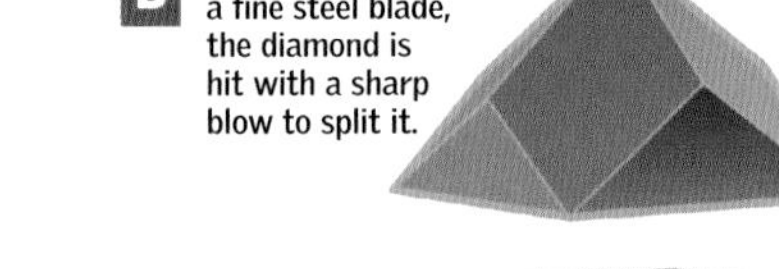

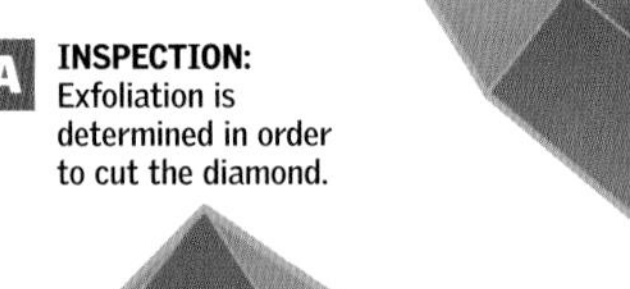

B CUTTING: Using a fine steel blade, the diamond is hit with a sharp blow to split it.

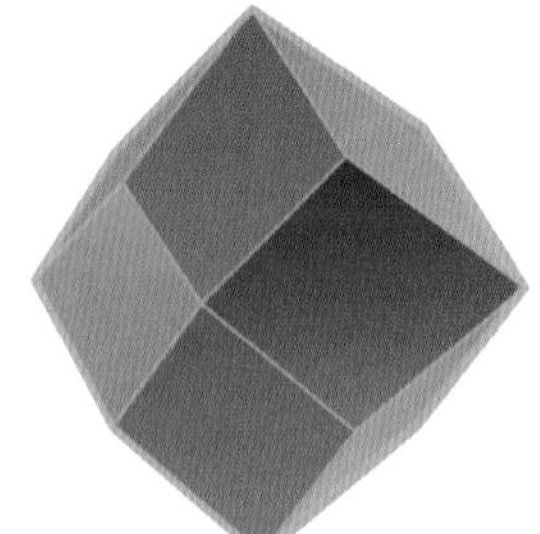

A INSPECTION: Exfoliation is determined in order to cut the diamond.

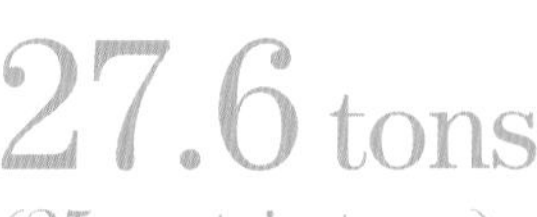

27.6 tons (25 metric tons) of mineral must be removed to obtain a **1 carat diamond.**

1 carat = 0.007 ounce (0.2 grams)

PRECIOUS STONES

DIAMOND
The presence of any color is due to chemical impurities.

EMERALD
Chromium gives it its characteristic green color.

OPAL
This amorphous silica substance has many colors.

RUBY
Its red color comes from chromium.

Gems

Mineral, rock, or petrified material that, after being cut and polished, is used in making jewelry. The cut and number of pieces that can be obtained is determined based on the particular mineral and its crystalline structure.

3 POLISHING

The shaping of the facets of the finished gem

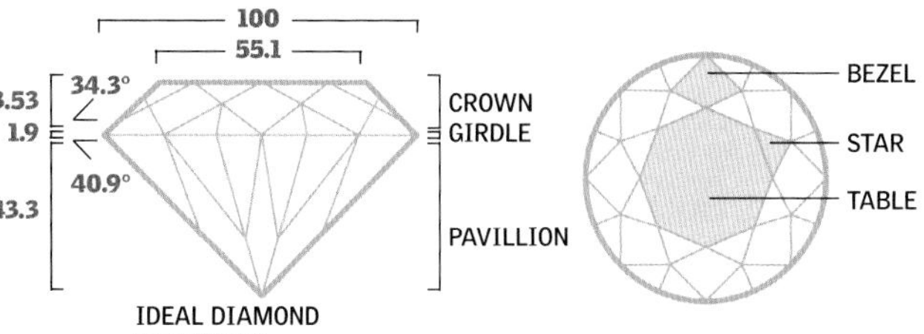

BRILLIANCE
The internal faces of the diamond act as mirrors because they are cut at exact angles and proportions.

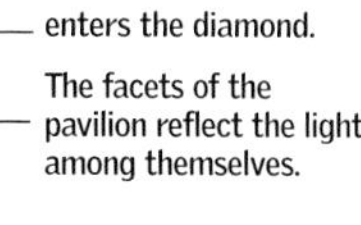

FIRE
Flashes of color from a well-cut diamond. Each ray of light is refracted into the colors of the rainbow.

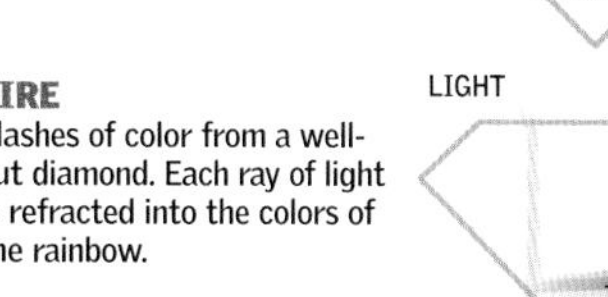

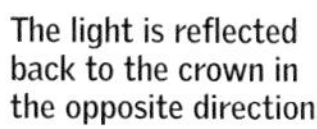

320 microns (0.32 mm)
MEASURED VERTICALLY

THE CHEMISTRY OF DIAMONDS

Strongly bonded carbon atoms crystallize in a cubic structure. Impurities or structural flaws can cause diamonds to show a hint of various colors, such as yellow, pink, green, and bluish white.

COMMON CUTS

A diamond can have many shapes, as long as its facets are carefully calculated to maximize its brilliance.

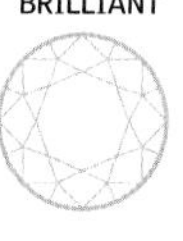
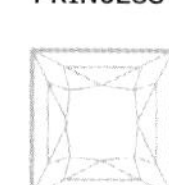
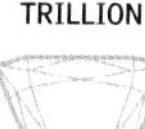

SEMIPRECIOUS STONES

SAPPHIRE
Blue to colorless corundum. They can also be yellow.

AMETHYST
Quartz whose color is determined by manganese and iron

TOPAZ
A gem of variable color, composed of silicon, aluminum, and fluorine

GARNET
A mix of iron, aluminum, magnesium, and vanadium

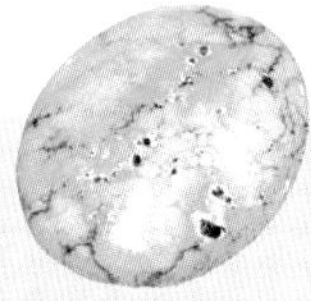

TURQUOISE
Aluminum phosphate and greenish blue copper

Diamonds in History

Diamonds are a sign of status, and their monetary value is determined by the law of supply and demand. First discovered by Hindus in 500 BC, diamonds gained fame in the early 20th century when they were advertised in the United States as the traditional gift from husbands to their wives. Some diamonds became famous, however, not only for their economic value but also for the tales and myths surrounding them.

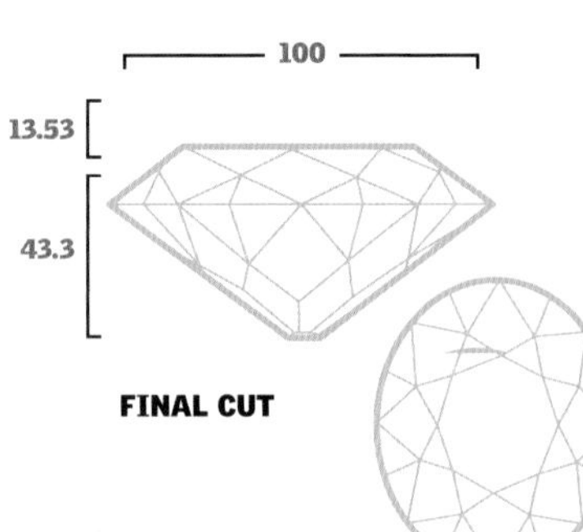

FINAL CUT

The Great Koh-i-noor Diamond

This diamond, which originated in India, now belongs to the British royal family. The raja of Malwa owned it for two centuries, until 1304, when it was stolen by the Mongols. In 1739 the Persians took possession of it. It witnessed bloody battles until finding its way back to India in 1813, after which point it reached the queen.

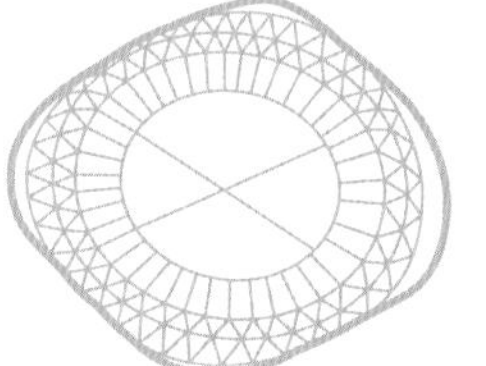

ORIGINAL CUT
It formerly weighed 186 carats with 30 facets that merged into six facets, which, in turn, became one. This explains its name: Mountain of Light.

Coronation of the Queen Mother

History

In 1856 this diamond was offered to Queen Victoria as compensation for the Sikh wars. She then had it recut. The Koh-i-noor was diminished to 109 carats.

ONLY FOR WOMEN
Because this diamond was believed to bring unhappiness to men, the superstitious Queen Victoria added a clause to her will stating that the diamond should only be handed down to the wives of future kings.

The Queen Mother's Crown

THE TAYLOR-BURTON DIAMOND
This diamond, with a weight of 69.42 carats, was auctioned in 1969. The day after buying it, Cartier sold it to the actor Richard Burton for $1.1 million. His wife Elizabeth Taylor tripled its value when she sold it after divorcing him.

Elizabeth Taylor

THE LEGEND OF THE VALLEY OF DIAMONDS
Alexander the Great introduced the legend of the Valley of Diamonds to Europe. According to this ancient account, later incorporated into the book *The Thousand and One Nights*, there was an inaccessible valley located in the mountains of northern India. The bed of this valley was covered with diamonds. To obtain them, raw meat was thrown in the valley and then fetched by trained birds, which would return it encrusted with diamonds.

The Misfortune of Possessing Hope

The Hope Diamond is legendary for the harm it brought to its owners since being stolen from the temple of the goddess Sita in India. According to the legend, its curse took lives and devoured fortunes. In 1949 diamond expert Harry Winston bought it and in 1958 donated it to the Smithsonian Institution, in Washington, D.C., where it can be viewed by the public.

Legend

Over the years, belief in the curse of the Hope Diamond was reinforced as its owners fell into ruin. Evalyn Walsh McLean, the last private owner of the diamond, did not sell it even after several tragedies befell her family.

1669	Louis XIV acquires the gem. He died in agony of gangrene.
1830	Henry Hope buys the diamond and suffers under the curse; he soon sells it.
1918	While the stone is in the hands of members of the McLean family, the patriarch and two of his daughters die.

Evalyn Walsh McLean

ORIGINAL CUT The purest of blue from the presence of boronic impurities, the diamond's color is also influenced by the presence of nitrogen, which adds a pale yellow shade.

Cullinan, the Greatest Find

Discovered in 1905 in South Africa, this diamond is the biggest ever found. It was sold to the government of Transvaal two years after its discovery for $300,000 (£150,000). It was then given to Edward VII on the occasion of his 66th birthday. The king entrusted the cutting of the diamond to Joseph Asscher of The Netherlands, who divided it into 105 pieces.

9 LARGE AND 96 SMALL PIECES
Joseph Asscher studied the huge stone for six months to decide how to cut it; he then divided it into nine primary stones and 96 smaller diamonds.

THE GREAT STAR OF AFRICA
This gem is the second largest cut diamond in the world, weighing 530 carats. Because it belongs to the British Crown, it is on display in the Tower of London.

FINAL CUT

530 carats

is the weight of the Cullinan I, the largest stone obtained from the original Cullinan find. It is followed by Cullinan II, which weighs 317 carats and is set in the imperial crown.

The Most Common Minerals

Silicates, which form 95 percent of the Earth's crust, are the most abundant type of mineral. Units of their tetrahedral structure, formed by the bonding of one silicon and four oxygen ions, combine to create several types of configurations, from isolated simple tetrahedrons to simple and double chains to sheets and three-dimensional complex networks. They can be light or dark; the latter have iron and magnesium in their chemical structures.

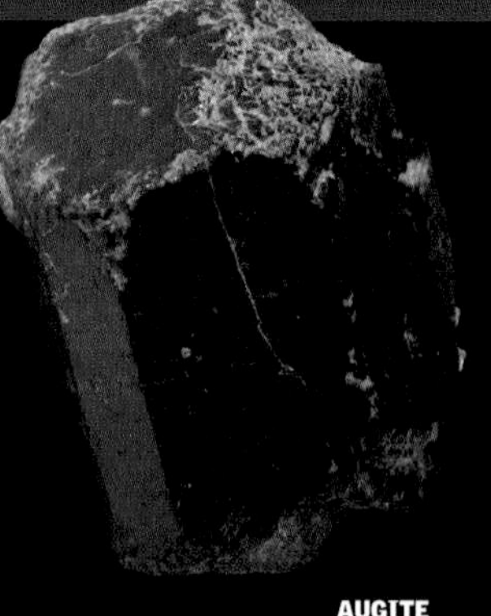

AUGITE

Structures

The basic unit of silicates consists of four oxygen ions located at the vertices of a tetrahedron, surrounding a silicon ion. Tetrahedrons can form by sharing oxygen ions, forming simple chains, laminar structures, or complex three-dimensional structures. The structural configuration also determines the type of exfoliation or fracture the silicate will exhibit: mica, which is composed of layers, exfoliates into flat sheets, whereas quartz fractures.

Simple Structure

All silicates have the same basic component: a silicon-oxygen tetrahedron. This structure consists of four oxygen ions that surround a much smaller silicon ion. Because this tetrahedron does not share oxygen ions with other tetrahedrons, it keeps its simple structure.

UNCOMBINED SILICATES

This group includes all silicates composed of independent tetrahedrons of silicon and oxygen. Example: olivine.

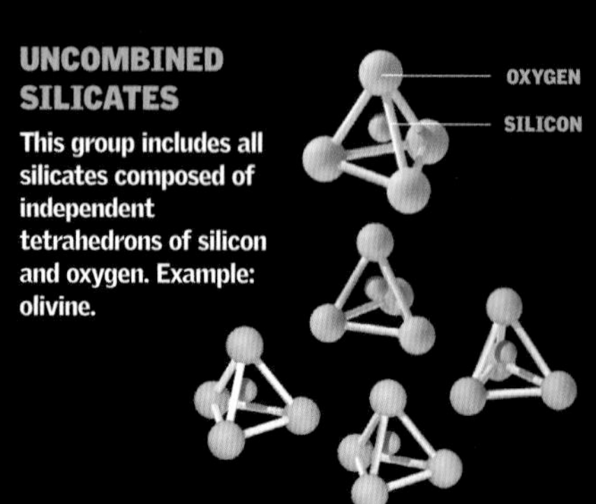

OLIVINE

Complex Structure

This structure occurs when the tetrahedrons share three of their four oxygen ions with neighboring tetrahedrons, spreading out to form a wide sheet. Because the strongest bonds are formed between silicon and oxygen, exfoliation runs in the direction of the other bonds, parallel to the sheets. There are several examples of this type of structure, but the most common ones are micas and clays. The latter can retain water within its sheets, which makes its size vary with hydration.

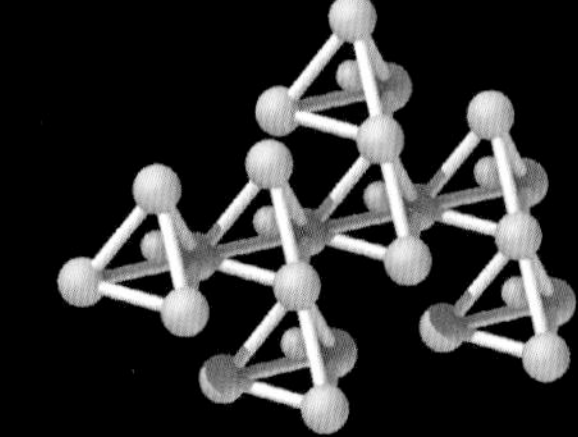

CHAINS

Clays are complex minerals with a very fine grain and a sheetlike structure.

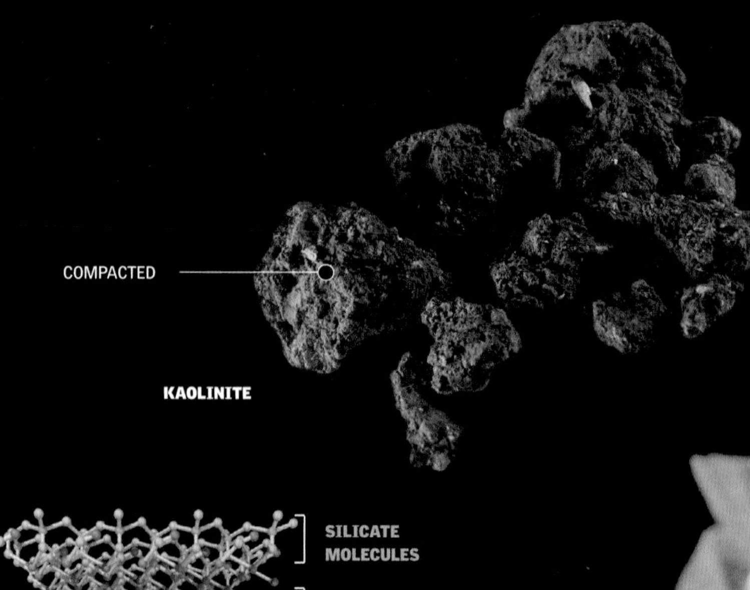

KAOLINITE

SILICATE MOLECULES

WATER MOLECULES

SILICATE MOLECULES

Three-dimensional Structure

Three fourths of the Earth's crust is composed of silicates with complex structures. Silicas, feldspars, feldspathoids, scapolites, and zeolites all have this type of structure. Their main characteristic is that their tetrahedrons share all their oxygen ions, forming a three-dimensional network with the same unitary composition. Quartz is part of the silica group.

LATERAL VIEW

THREE-DIMENSIONAL STRUCTURE

Quartz has a complex three-dimensional structure composed only of silicon and oxygen.

VIEW FROM ABOVE

MINERAL COMBINATIONS

DARK SILICATES

IRON AND MAGNESIUM
EXAMPLE: BIOTITE

The color and heaviness of this mineral are caused by the presence of iron and magnesium ions. Known as a ferromagnesian mineral, biotite's specific gravity varies between 3.2 and 3.6.

Iron is added to its composition.

LIGHT SILICATES

MAGNESIUM
EXAMPLE: MINERAL TALC

This mineral contains variable amounts of calcium, aluminum, sodium, and potassium. Its specific gravity is, on average, 2.7—much lower than that of ferromagnesian minerals.

Calcium is added to its composition.

CA

RESULTING SHAPE

The quartz crystal maintains a hexagonal shape with its six sides converging to a tip (pyramid).

A CRYSTAL OF GREAT VOLUME

For a quartz crystal to acquire large dimensions, it needs a great deal of silicon and oxygen, much time, and ample space.

The Nonsilicates

Sulfurs, oxides, sulfates, pure elements, carbonates, hydroxides, and phosphates are less abundant than silicates in the Earth's crust. They make up eight percent of minerals, but they are very important economically. They are also important components of rock. Since ancient times, some have been appreciated for their usefulness or simply for their beauty. Others are still being researched for possible industrial uses.

Very Few in a Pure State

It is rare for native chemical elements to be found in the Earth's crust in a pure state. In general, they must be extracted from other minerals by means of industrial chemical processes. However, they can occasionally be found in rocks in a pure state. Diamonds, for instance, are pure carbon.

Native Elements

In addition to carbon—which forms minerals such as diamond and graphite when crystallized—copper, gold, sulfur, silver, and platinum are other minerals that are found as native elements.

ASSOCIATION
The greenish color indicates the formation of copper sulfate.

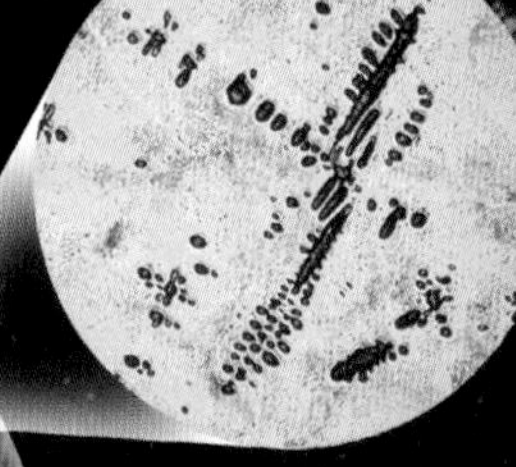

DENDRITES
Microscopic forms that appear when copper solidifies and crystallizes

FORMATION OF CHALCOPYRITE
Iron, copper, and sulfur are present.

COPPER

1.2 inches (3 CM)

Copper nuggets can reach a high degree of purity.

MAGNETITE

Oxides

Metal associations with oxygen atoms. Ilmenite, hematite, and chromite are ores from which titanium, iron, and chrome are extracted. Rubies and sapphires are extracted from corundum.

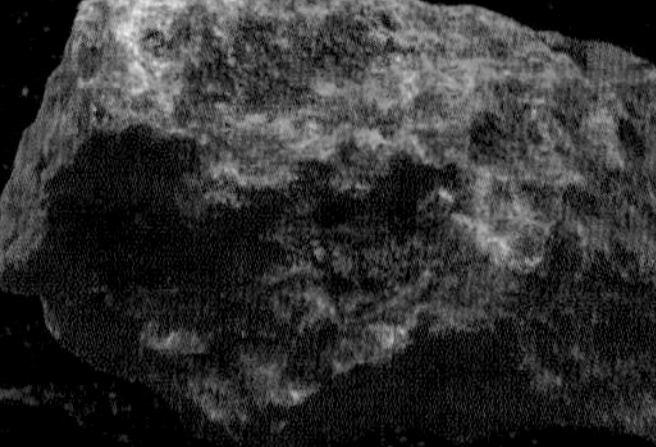

LIMONITE

Hydroxides

Known in chemical terms as a base, these types of minerals appear through the association of oxide with water. Limonite, an iron ore used as pigment because of its reddish color, and bauxite (or aluminum hydroxide) are among the most abundant hydroxides. Bauxite is the ore from which aluminum, a metal that is becoming more and more widely used, is extracted.

APATITE

Phosphates

Both apatite, used as fertilizer, and the semiprecious stone turquoise are phosphates. These materials have a complex structure based on an ion composed of one phosphorus and four oxygen atoms. These ions, in turn, are associated with compound ions of other elements.

In Alloys and Compounds

As was the case with silicates, it is very difficult to find rocks composed of pure nonsilicate elements—elements with atoms of only one type. The constituent elements of nature, metal and nonmetal, tend to join together and form compounds and alloys. From a chemical perspective, even ice, solidified water, is a compound of hydrogen and oxygen atoms. Some compounds are used as ores, meaning that they are mined for their constituent elements. For example, pure aluminum is obtained from bauxite. Other compound minerals, however, are used for their specific properties, which can be very different from those of each of their constituent elements. This is the case with magnetite, which is an iron oxide.

MALACHITE

Carbonates

Simpler than silicates, minerals in this group are composed of a complex anion associated with a positive ion. Calcium carbonate (calcite, the main component of limestone) and calcium magnesium carbonate (dolomite) are the most common carbonates.

FLUORITE

Halides

are binary compounds. One halite is table salt (or sodium chloride). Halites have many uses: fluorite is used in the industrial production of steel, and sylvite (potassium chloride) is used as fertilizer.

GYPSUM ROSETTE

Sulfates

Gypsum, widely used in construction, is a calcium sulfate that forms in the sea and contains water in its structure. Without water, calcium sulfate forms another mineral, anhydrite, which is also used in construction. Barytine is a sulfate from which the metal barium is extracted.

ENCRUSTED IN ROCK

Here crystals are encrusted in slate, a metamorphic rock.

"FOOL'S GOLD"
was an early name for pyrite because of its glitter.

0.04 inch (1 mm)

PYRITE

Sulfides

are found in metal ores and are associated with sulfur. Examples of sulfides are pyrite (iron), chalcopyrite (iron and copper), argentite (silver), cinnabar (mercury), galena (lead), and sphalerite (zinc).

STRUCTURE OF PYRITE

The cubic shape of crystals comes from the balanced location of iron and sulfur atoms.

Formation and Transformation of Rocks

Natural forces create an incredible variety of landscapes, such as deserts, beaches, elevated peaks, ravines, canyons, and underground caves. Settings like the one in the picture amaze us and arouse our interest in finding out what is hidden in the cave's depths. Rocks subjected to high pressure and temperatures can

SUBTERRANEAN WORLD
This awe-inspiring limestone cave in Neversink Pit (Alabama) looks like no other place on Earth.

ROCKS OF FIRE 42-43
SCULPTED VALLEY 44-45
EVERYTHING CHANGES 46-49
DARK AND DEEP 50-51
IF STONES COULD SPEAK 52-53
METAMORPHIC PROCESSES 54-55
THE BASIS OF LIFE 56-57
DIVINE AND WORSHIPED 58-59

undergo remarkable changes. An initially igneous rock can become sedimentary and later metamorphic. There are experts who overcome every type of obstacle to reach inhospitable places, even in the bowels of the Earth, in search of strange or precious materials, such as gold and silver. They also look for fossils to learn about life-forms and environments of the past. ●

Rocks of Fire

Igneous (from Latin *ignis*, "fire") rocks form when magma coming from the rocky mantle (underneath the crust) rises, cools, and solidifies. When magma comes to the surface as lava and solidifies relatively quickly, it creates extrusive rocks, such as basalt or rhyolite. On the other hand, when magma seeps into caves or between rock layers and slowly solidifies, intrusive igneous rocks, such as gabbro and granite, are formed. These rocks usually have thicker grains and are less dense than the extrusive ones. They are arranged in structures called dikes, sills, and batholiths beneath the surface. Igneous rocks make up most of the Earth's crust. ●

A Complex Process

The Earth's crust is 44 miles (70 km) deep at most. Farther down, rocks are molten or semimolten, forming magma that rises through the crust and opens paths through cracks, cavities, or volcanoes. Magma can solidify when it is moving or still or when underground or expelled to the surface. All these characteristics together with different mineral compositions create a wide variety of igneous rocks.

CRUST
Rigid, outermost layer

ROCKY MANTLE
1,800 miles (2,900 km) thick

CORE
The outer core is made of solid iron and melted nickel.

PYROCLASTS
Rock fragments and ash that spread out over miles

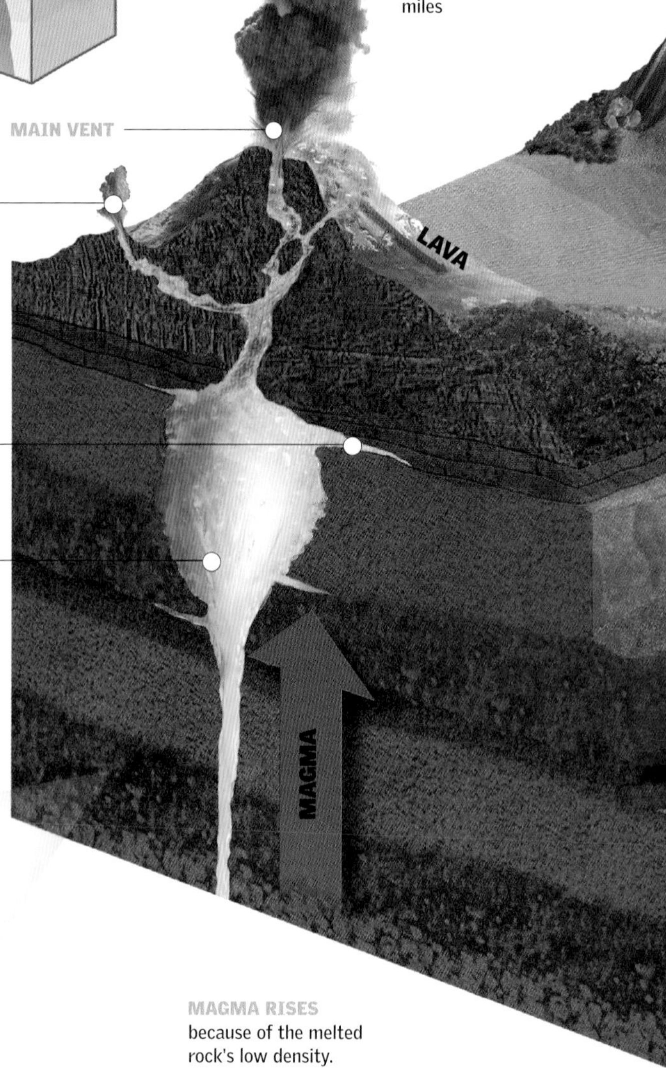

LATERAL VENTS

2,200° F (1,200° C)

THE TEMPERATURE OF LAVA IN THE CRUST

SILLS
occupy the spaces between overlying layers of rocks.

MAGMA CHAMBER
receives magma material from the mantle.

MAGMA RISES
because of the melted rock's low density.

BENEATH THE SURFACE
PLUTONIC ROCKS

Most magma is underground in the form of plutons, which undergo a solidification process. This forms intrusive (or plutonic) rocks. When magma intrudes into vertical fissures, the resulting rock formations are called dikes; those between sedimentary layers are sills; and batholiths are masses hundreds of miles long. In general, intrusive rocks crystallize slowly, and their minerals form thick grains. But the solidification process will determine the structure; the rock will be different depending on whether solidification is slow (over millions of years) or fast and whether it loses or gains materials along the way.

GRANITE
Composed of feldspar and quartz crystals, it is rich in sodium, potassium, and silica.

70% SILICA CONTENT

DIKES

The structure of the rock depends on its formation process. Thus, a rock resulting from magma intrusion into a dike will have a structure and coloring different from the rock around it because of having crystallized faster.

SURROUNDING ROCK

INTRUSIVE ROCK

ON THE SURFACE
VOLCANIC ROCK

Volcanic, or extrusive, rocks are those that reach the surface as lava because of volcanic activity. They solidify relatively quickly on the surface. Some, like the obsidians, solidify too quickly to crystallize. This class of rock is distinguished by its viscosity, caused by the low silica content and dissolved gas at the moment of eruption, which give these rocks a particular texture. Highly liquid lava, such as basalt, usually covers large surfaces because it solidifies on the outside while still remaining fluid underground.

BASALT ROCK originates from highly liquid fluid magma that cools quickly.

50% **SILICA CONTENT** According to the type of lava

ASH CONE Composed of pyroclasts of the volcano itself

LACCOLITH is located between superficial layers.

DIKE Formed by magma that intruded into a vertical fracture

PLATEAU Composed of rhyolitic volcanic lava (rich in silicon)

CALDERA Collapsed volcanic crater covered with water

BRANCHING LACCOLITH

VOLCANIC OUTCROPPING

ERODED LAVA FLOW

SOLID ROCK

LAKE

MUD FLATS

2,550° F (1,400° C)

MAGMA TEMPERATURE AT A DEPTH OF 125 MILES (200 KM)

STOCKS are massive plutons smaller than batholiths.

BATHOLITH can be an old magma chamber that has solidified over thousands of years.

Bowen's Reaction Series

Different magma materials solidify at different temperatures. Minerals with calcium, iron, and magnesium crystallize first, giving them a dark coloring (olivine, pyroxene). But sodium, potassium, and aluminum crystallize at lower temperatures, remaining in the residual magma until the end of the process. They are present only in pale-colored rock, which crystallizes later. Sometimes different stages of the process can be seen in the same rock.

AGATE ROCK

LAST LAYER TO CRYSTALLIZE

RICH IN SODIUM

COOLING OF MAGMA

FIRST LAYER TO CRYSTALLIZE

RICH IN CALCIUM

Sculpted Valley

Yosemite National Park is located 200 miles (320 km) east of San Francisco, California. This park is known worldwide for its granite cliffs, waterfalls, crystalline rivers, and forests of giant sequoias. It covers an area of 1,190 square miles (3,081 sq km) and extends along the eastern slopes of the Sierra Nevada range. Yosemite National Park has over three million visitors every year.

103 Million Years

EL CAPITAN
300-foot-high (1,000 m) granite cliff used for mountain climbing

Yosemite

This park has an average elevation of 1,300 to 2,000 feet (400-600 m) above sea level. The geology of the area is mostly composed of a granitic batholith, but five percent of the park is composed of formations from the metamorphism of volcanic and sedimentary rocks. Erosion at different elevations and fracture systems created valleys, canyons, hills, and other current geological formations. The wide separation between fractures and joints is caused by the amount of silica present in the granite and in the metamorphic rocks.

FORMATION OF THE LANDSCAPE

Erosion in the joints resulted in valleys and canyons. The strongest erosive forces of the last several million years have been glaciers, which changed the V-shaped valleys created by rivers into U-shaped glacial valleys.

1 BATHOLITH FORMATION
Almost all rocky formations at Yosemite Park are composed of granite; they belong to the original batholith.

GRANITE

2 ASCENT
Ten million years ago, the Sierra Nevada underwent a tectonic elevation that caused the batholith to emerge.

ELEVATION

V-SHAPED SLOPES

3 EROSION
One million years ago, the descending flow of glacial ice gave the valley a U shape.

U-SHAPED CANYONS

GLACIATION

YOSEMITE NATIONAL PARK

United States

Latitude 37° N

Longitude 119° W

Location	**California**
Surface	**1,190 square miles (3,081 sq km)**
Visitors in 2005	**3,380,038**
Opened on	**9/25/1890**
Administered by	**National Park Service**

CASCADES

Some rock formations in the park serve as platforms for waterfalls, especially in April, May, and June when the snow melts upstream. The valley has nine waterfalls, five of which are over 1,000 feet (300 m) high; Yosemite Falls is 2,600 feet (800 m) high. This is the highest waterfall in North America and the third highest in the world.

103 Million Years Ago

CATHEDRAL ROCKS
One of the main rock formations, with compacted and scratched granite walls

87 Million Years Ago

HALF DOME
Granite monolith of unique beauty. It is lower than El Capitan, being 2,160 feet (660 m) high.

616 feet (188 m)

FREE FALL

BRIDAL VEIL FALLS
This huge waterfall formed as a consequence of glacial thaw in a "hanging" valley.

FOREST
The park has three groves of giant sequoias, among other species.

FISSURES

The erosion at rock joints causes fissures within them, and this process leads to the formation of valleys and canyons. The downward flow of the glacial mass of ice cut and sculpted the valley into a U shape. Today this unique landscape attracts great numbers of visitors.

ROCK
Compact granite forming a large batholith

FISSURE
Produced by erosion at rock joints

Everything Changes

Wind, ice, and water. These natural elements cause great changes in the Earth's landscape. Erosion and transportation are processes that produce and spread rock materials. Then, when these materials settle and become compacted, new rocks are created, which in turn will revert to sediment. These are sedimentary rocks: the most widely known rocks, they cover 70 percent of the Earth's surface. By observing sedimentary rocks of different ages, scientists can estimate how the climate and the environment have changed. ●

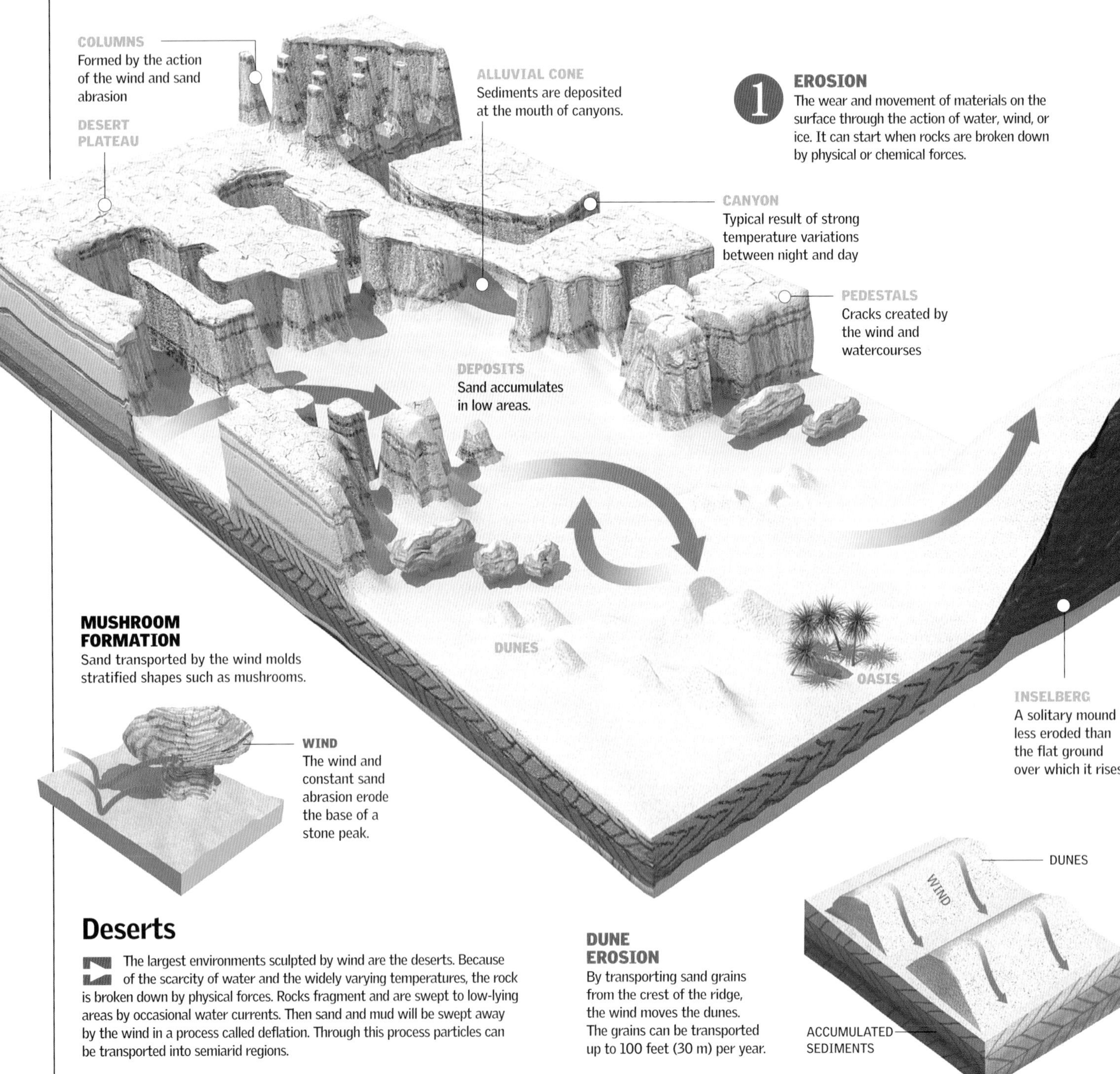

Deserts

The largest environments sculpted by wind are the deserts. Because of the scarcity of water and the widely varying temperatures, the rock is broken down by physical forces. Rocks fragment and are swept to low-lying areas by occasional water currents. Then sand and mud will be swept away by the wind in a process called deflation. Through this process particles can be transported into semiarid regions.

DUNE EROSION

By transporting sand grains from the crest of the ridge, the wind moves the dunes. The grains can be transported up to 100 feet (30 m) per year.

TRANSPORT OF SEDIMENTS

DESERT
TINY GRAINS
In the desert, the wind moves particles in three ways: suspension (very fine grains and dust), transport (the most basic way), and sliding along the surface.

SAND

WIND

3 INCHES (10 CM)

GLACIER
FINE AND HETEROGENEOUS
Glaciers transport rock fragments, which accumulate in moraines. They are made up of a heterogeneous material called till, which, together with rocks, is carried along by the glacier.

ICE

TILL

160 FEET (50 M)

GLACIAL CIRQUE
At the upper end of the valley, the walls erode in a semicircular form.

2 TRANSPORT

After erosion, fragments are transported to an area where they will be deposited. In deserts, the wind transports the sand grains, forming dunes; with glaciers, the debris forms frontal and lateral moraines.

SLOPES
Rocks fall from slopes onto glaciers. They are included in the material that makes up the moraine.

CENTRAL MORAINE
forms when two valley glaciers meet, creating only one mass of ice.

CRACKS

TRANSPORTED ROCK
will be deposited on the moraines.

LATERAL MORAINE
Formed by the fragments accumulated along the sides of the glacier

ERRATICS
are large rock fragments that the glacier transports and deposits.

FINE SEDIMENT
is deposited under the glacier and at its front end. The deposited material is called till.

U-SHAPED VALLEYS
Glaciers erode valleys, forming a U shape because erosion is greatest at the bottom.

GLACIER
Mass of ice that flows down over a landmass.

Glaciers

These huge ice masses form on the ground, slowly moving downward through the action of gravity. As they advance, they carry away rocks in their path. At the head of a glacier valley, the walls erode in a semicircle, forming what is called a glacial cirque. The simultaneous, progressive erosion of the walls creates a pyramidal horn, or peak. The valleys through which a glacier has passed are U-shaped instead of the V shape typical of the erosion of river valleys.

TERMINAL MORAINE
Rocks that fall onto the glacier, along with the rock it was already carrying, accumulate at the front of the glacier and form what is called a terminal moraine.

GLACIER

ICE

ACCUMULATED SEDIMENTS

TRANSPORT OF SEDIMENTS

RIVER
GREAT DISTANCES
A river can transport sediments over great distances. Rivers originate in elevated areas, from which they flow to lower areas and then to the sea. When the current gathers speed, it transports big boulders. When the energy is less, the current carries only smaller rocks.

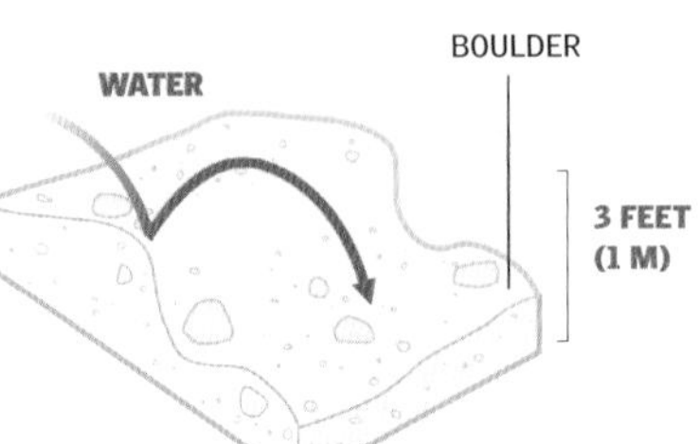

COAST
LOCAL DEPOSITS
After each wave breaks, the undertow descends the beach slope, creating an accumulation of sand that has been transported by the waves in a process called a coastal current. Sand is also transported by rivers, which deposit sediments in their deltas.

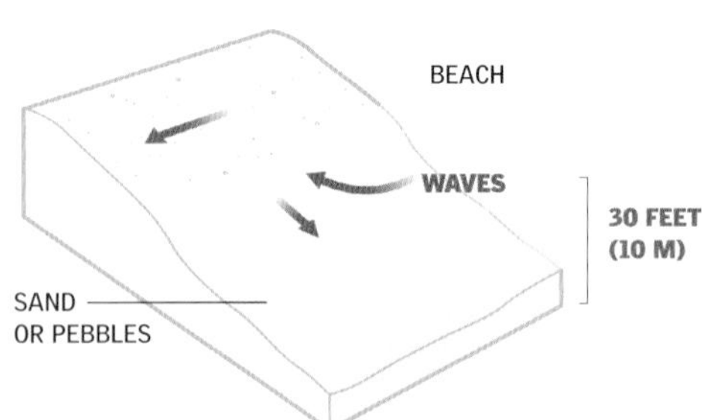

WATERFALLS
Softer rock erodes, forming a cave with a rocky ceiling that will finally crumble and fall.

3 SEDIMENTATION

When the currents that transport sediment lose energy, the sediment is deposited in layers and distributed over extensive areas.

SLOPE
River valleys are steep because they are composed of layers of hard rock.

CLIFF
A product of lateral undermining

RAPIDS
In these geographic features, a high volume of matter is transported by river erosion.

MEANDERS
The outside of the curve is where the most sediment is deposited.

FORMATION OF V-SHAPED VALLEYS
Unlike glacial valleys, which are eroded in the shape of a U, river valleys are V-shaped.

ALLUVIAL PLAIN
Composed of sediments

RIVER
Close to the river's source, the current is very strong, and it erodes and digs into the riverbed to form V-shaped valleys.

Rivers

Close to their source, rivers flow through areas of high elevation. The water descends there with great force and energy, which enables the current to transport large boulders. At low elevations, rivers flow more smoothly over sediments, forming meanders and eroding laterally. On reaching the coast, rivers deposit sediments and form estuaries or deltas.

DELTA FORMATION
The sediment deposited at the river's mouth creates a delta, an area with sandbars through which the river flows in various directions.

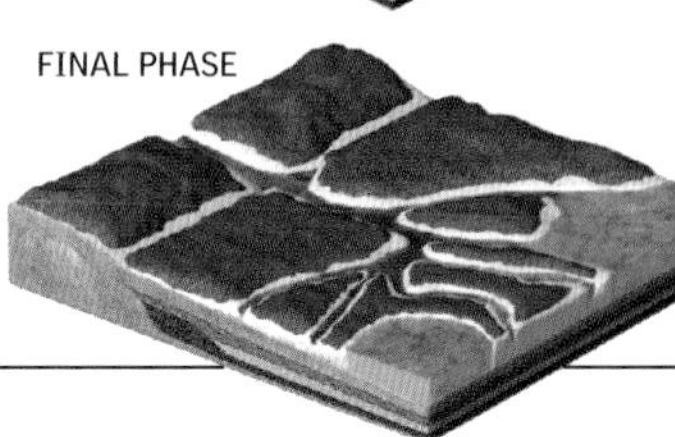

CEMENTATION PROCESS

This is the most important process that transforms sediment into rock. Cementation occurs when particles join with the materials precipitated from the water currents. Sedimentary rocks are formed through the union of different minerals that have been dissolved in water. When the water evaporates or cools, the dissolved minerals can precipitate and form deposits that accumulate with other sediments, or they can form rocks on their own. Salts and sandstone are common examples of cemented rocks.

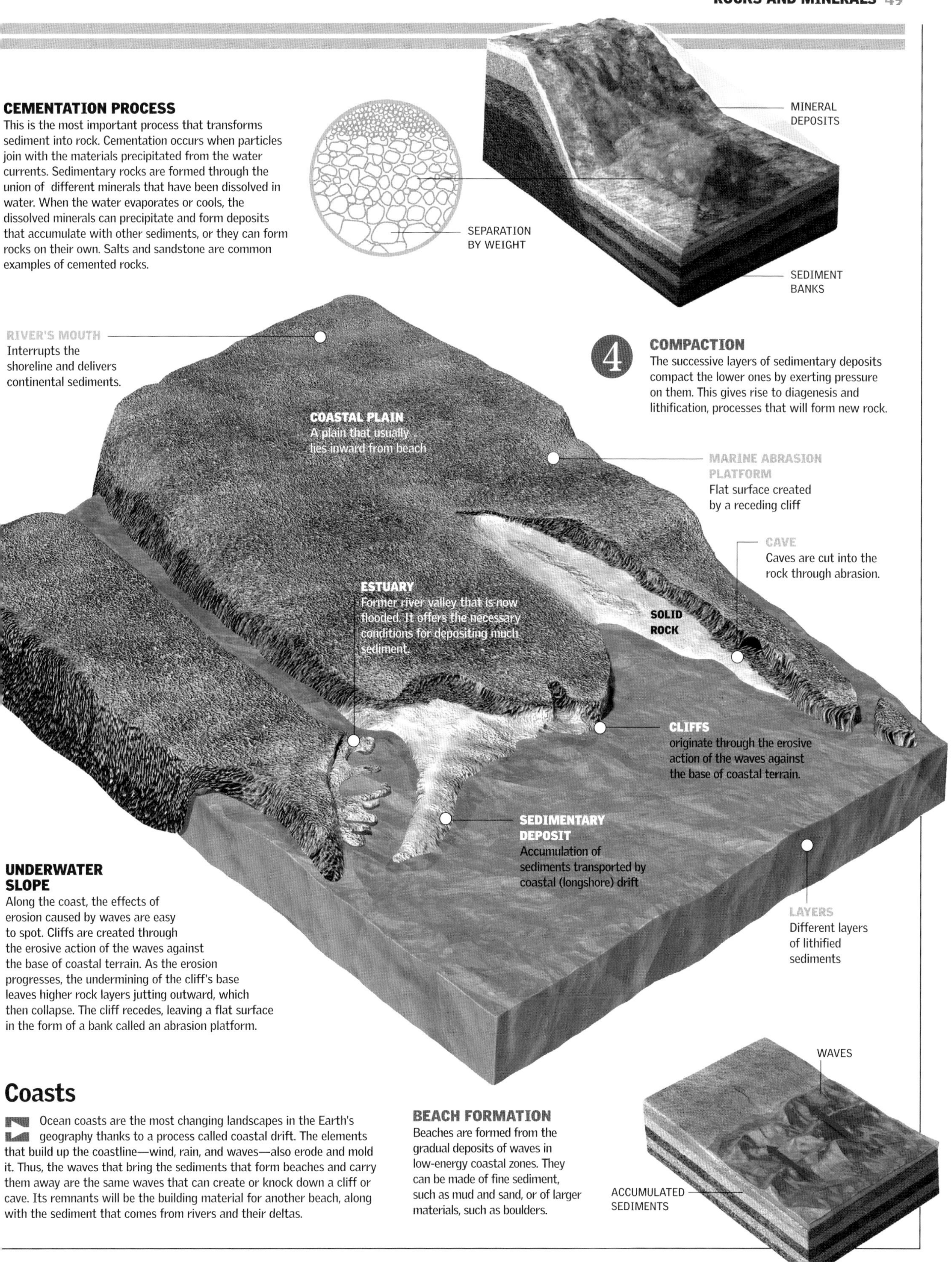

4 COMPACTION

The successive layers of sedimentary deposits compact the lower ones by exerting pressure on them. This gives rise to diagenesis and lithification, processes that will form new rock.

UNDERWATER SLOPE

Along the coast, the effects of erosion caused by waves are easy to spot. Cliffs are created through the erosive action of the waves against the base of coastal terrain. As the erosion progresses, the undermining of the cliff's base leaves higher rock layers jutting outward, which then collapse. The cliff recedes, leaving a flat surface in the form of a bank called an abrasion platform.

Coasts

Ocean coasts are the most changing landscapes in the Earth's geography thanks to a process called coastal drift. The elements that build up the coastline—wind, rain, and waves—also erode and mold it. Thus, the waves that bring the sediments that form beaches and carry them away are the same waves that can create or knock down a cliff or cave. Its remnants will be the building material for another beach, along with the sediment that comes from rivers and their deltas.

BEACH FORMATION

Beaches are formed from the gradual deposits of waves in low-energy coastal zones. They can be made of fine sediment, such as mud and sand, or of larger materials, such as boulders.

Dark and Deep

A cave is a hollow space created essentially through the chemical action of water on a soluble, usually chalky, material. Caves have three structures: stalactites (conical structures that hang from the cave ceiling), stalagmites (structures that jut from the cave floor), and columns (created when stalactites and stalagmites join). The cycle of cave formation is called the karst cycle, which lasts a total of around one million years. For this reason, young, active caves have noisy streams and cascades, whereas old caves are silent wonders decorated with stalagmites, stalactites, and columns.

The Karst Cycle

When water dissolves high calcium content rock through the corrosive effect of carbonic acid, it forms networks of conduits and galleries. The initial fissures widen not only through this chemical process but also mechanically through the abrasive action of pebbles and other insoluble elements. Water is filtered until it reaches lower levels, leaving in its wake openings arranged in levels and separated by vertical pits and passages that connect the different levels.

1 STRUCTURE OF THE STRATUM OF A CAVE
The ground's original structure is composed of permeable limestone. It has fissures through which river or rainwater is filtered. This starts the erosive process.

2 INITIAL CAVE
Water, following the contour of the terrain, forms an underground river. The first calcite or calcium carbonate deposits start to form in the shape of stalactites.

3 EXTENDED CAVE SYSTEM
Formed when several tunnels are joined together. Sometimes the surface of the soil starts to sink, creating sinkholes. If the cave extends below the water table, tunnels are formed.

COLUMN
If stalactites and stalagmites grow until they join together, they become columns.

130 feet
(39 m)
THE HIGHEST COLUMN IN THE WORLD

STALAGMITE
Water droplets containing dissolved carbonate create stalagmites as they drip down.

100 feet
(30 m)
THE TALLEST STALAGMITE IN THE WORLD

Stalactite Formation

Limestone is a rock composed almost exclusively of calcium carbonate, which dissolves in naturally acid water. Rainwater absorbs carbon dioxide from the air and microorganisms from the ground, becoming a weak acid. When filtered, it can dissolve limestone over time. If this water drips into a cave, it loses carbon dioxide to the air and deposits the excess calcium in stalactites and stalagmites, thereby maintaining chemical equilibrium. Stalactites are excellent examples of chemical sedimentary rocks.

65º F
(18º C)

IDEAL TEMPERATURE FOR THE PRECIPITATION OF CARBONATE

Water Droplet

1 **WATER DROPLET** Every stalactite starts from a simple water droplet containing dissolved salts.

2 **CALCITE** When the droplet falls, it leaves behind a narrow calcite trail.

3 **MORE LAYERS** Each successive droplet that falls deposits another fine calcite layer.

4 **INTERIOR TUBE** The layers form around a narrow pipe (0.02 inch [0.5 mm]) through which the water seeps.

5 **STALACTITE** If many droplets are deposited over this pipe, stalactites are formed.

STALACTITES can form on ceilings and cement floors, although they form much faster in a cave's natural environment that contains carbon-rich solutions.

23 feet
(7 m)

THE BIGGEST STALACTITE IN THE WORLD

CANGO CAVES SOUTH AFRICA

Latitude 33º S
Longitude 18º E

Length	3.3 miles (5.3 km)
Depth	200 feet (60 m)
Location	East of Cape Town

Other Formations

A passing underground current forms two types of landscape: canyons and tunnels. Underground rivers and waterfalls above the water table create deep, undulating canyons by eroding and dissolving limestone and by abrading the rock layers with sediment. Below the water table, caves are full of water that moves slowly, dissolving walls, floors, and ceilings of carbonate rock to create tunnels.

CANGO CAVES

Isolated in a narrow strip of limestone from the Precambrian, in the highlands of Oudtshoorn, the Cango Caves are remarkable for their abundant deposits of calcite. They are left over from a larger channel below the water table. This channel dried up when the neighboring surface valleys were worn down to lower levels. The impressive stalagmites were then formed..

If Stones Could Speak

Rock strata form from sediments deposited over time in successive layers. Sometimes these sediments bury remains of organisms that can later become fossils, which provide key data about the environment and prehistoric life on Earth. The geologic age of rocks and the processes they have undergone can be discovered through different methods that combine analyses of successive layers and the fossils they contain. ●

GRAND CANYO
Colorado River
Arizona
Latitude 36° N
Length 112° W

CONTINUITY

The Grand Canyon tells the history of the Earth in colorful layers on its walls. The Colorado River has been carving its way through the plateau for six million years. The layers along the river provide an uninterrupted account of geological history.

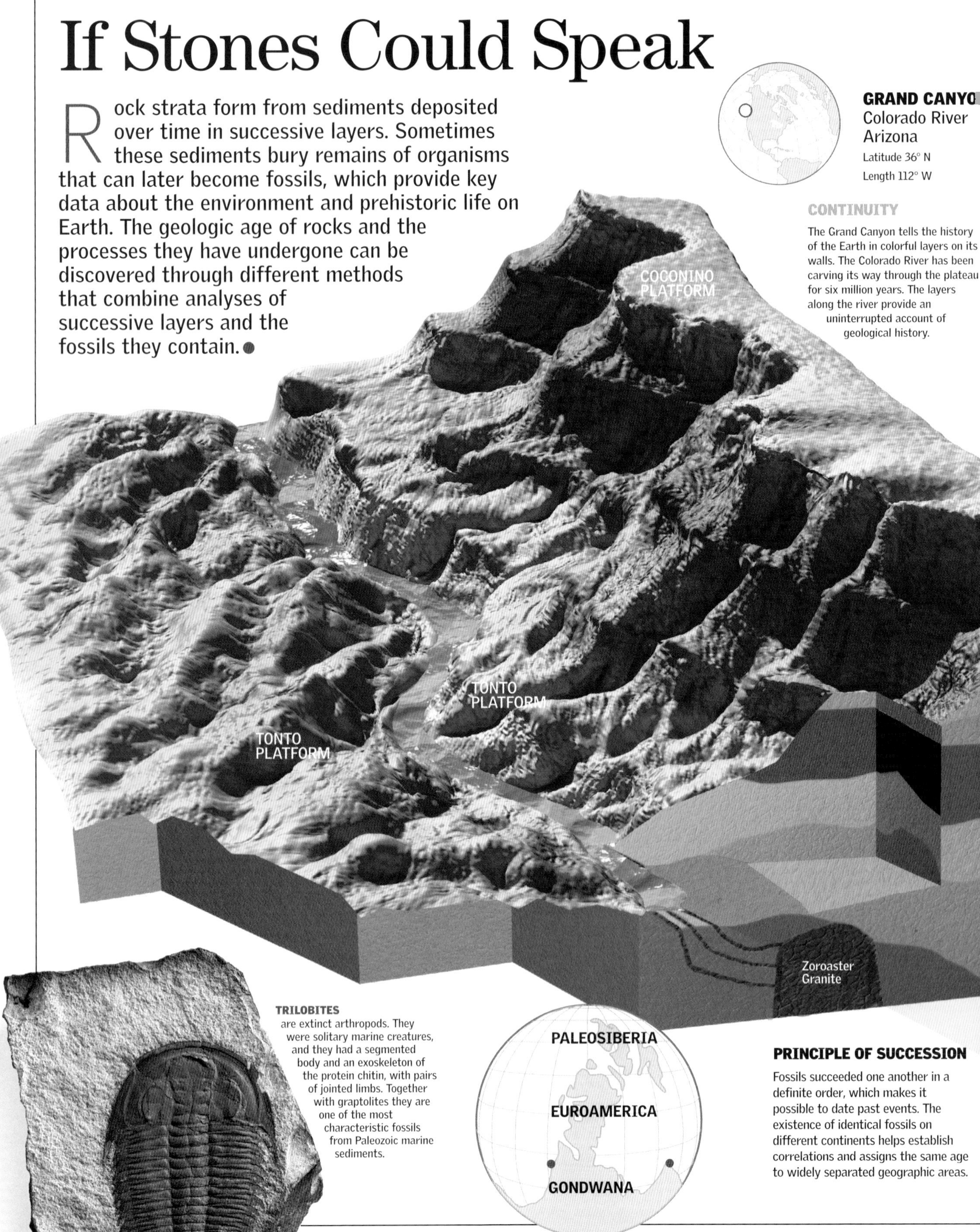

TRILOBITES are extinct arthropods. They were solitary marine creatures, and they had a segmented body and an exoskeleton of the protein chitin, with pairs of jointed limbs. Together with graptolites they are one of the most characteristic fossils from Paleozoic marine sediments.

PRINCIPLE OF SUCCESSION

Fossils succeeded one another in a definite order, which makes it possible to date past events. The existence of identical fossils on different continents helps establish correlations and assigns the same age to widely separated geographic areas.

1. When it dies, an animal can be submerged on a riverbed, protected from oxygen. The body begins to decompose.

2. The skeleton is completely covered with sediments. Over the years, new layers are added, burying the earlier layers.

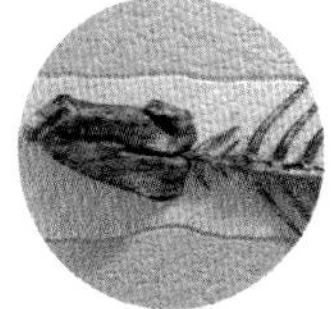

During fossilization, molecules of the original tissue are replaced precisely with minerals that petrify it.

A Fossil's Age

Fossils are remains of organisms that lived in the past. Today scientists use several procedures, including carbon-14 dating, to estimate their age. This method makes it possible to date organic remains with precision from as long ago as 60,000 years. If organisms are older, there are other methods for absolute dating. However, within a known area, a fossil's location in a given sedimentary layer enables scientists to place it on an efficient, relative time scale. Following principles of original horizontality and of succession, it is possible to find out when an organism lived.

3. Once the water disappears, the fossil is already formed and crystallized. The crust's movements raise the layers, bringing the fossil to the surface.

4. Erosion exposes the fossil to full view. With carbon-14 dating, scientists can determine if it is less than 60,000 years old.

Rock Layers and the Passage of Time

Rock layers are essential for time measurement because they retain information not only about the geologic past but also about past life-forms, climate, and more. The principle of original horizontality establishes that the layers of sediment are deposited horizontally and parallel to the surface and that they are defined by two planes that show lateral continuity. If layers are folded or bent, they must have been altered by some geologic process. These ruptures are called unconformities. If the continuity between layers is interrupted, it means that there was an interval of time and, consequently, erosion in the layer below. This also is called unconformity, since it interrupts the horizontality principle.

Period
PERMIAN
CARBONIFEROUS
DEVONIAN
CAMBRIAN
PRECAMBRIAN

Cononino Sandstone
Hermit Shale
Muav Limestone
Bright Angel Shale

SUPAI GROUP
Paraconformity
REDWALL LIMESTONE
460 feet (140 m)
Disconformity
TONTO GROUP
1,000 feet (310 m)
Angular Unconformity
Unconformity
UNKAR GROUP
Colorado River
VISHNU SCHISTS

TEMPORAL HIATUS

Unconformity between the Tonto Group and the Redwall Limestone indicates a temporal hiatus. Between the Redwall Limestone and the Supai Group, there is temporal continuity.

Metamorphic Processes

When rocks are subjected to certain conditions (high pressure and temperature or exposure to fluids with dissolved chemicals), they can undergo remarkable changes in both their mineral composition and their structure. This very slow process, called metamorphism, is a veritable transformation of the rock. This phenomenon originates inside the Earth's crust as well as on the surface. The type of metamorphism depends on the nature of the energy that triggers the change. This energy can be heat or pressure. ●

SCOTLAND,
United Kingdom
Latitude 57° N
Longitude 04° W

Scotland was raised in the Caledonian orogeny 400 million years ago. This pressure produced the gneiss shown in the photo.

Dynamic Metamorphism

The least common type of metamorphism, dynamic metamorphism happens when the large-scale movement of the crust along fault systems causes the rocks to be compressed. Great rock masses thrust over others. Where they come in contact new metamorphic rocks, called cataclasites and mylonites, are formed.

Slate
In environments with high temperature and pressure, slates will become phyllites.

570° F
(300° C)

SLATE
Metamorphic rock of low grade that forms through pressure at about 390° F (200° C). It becomes more compact and dense.

930° F
(500° C)

SCHIST
Very flaky rock produced by metamorphism at intermediate temperatures and depths greater than six miles (10 km). The minerals recrystallize.

1,200° F
(650° C)

GNEISS
Produced through highly metamorphic processes more than 12 miles (20 km) beneath the surface, it involves extremely powerful tectonic forces and temperatures near the melting point of rock.

1,470° F
(800° C)

FUSION
At this temperature, most rocks start to melt until they become liquid.

Regional Metamorphism

As mountains form, a large amount of rock is deformed and transformed. Rocks buried close to the surface descend to greater depths and are modified by higher temperatures and pressures. This metamorphism covers thousands of square miles and is classified according to the temperature and pressure reached. Slate is an example of rock affected by this type of process.

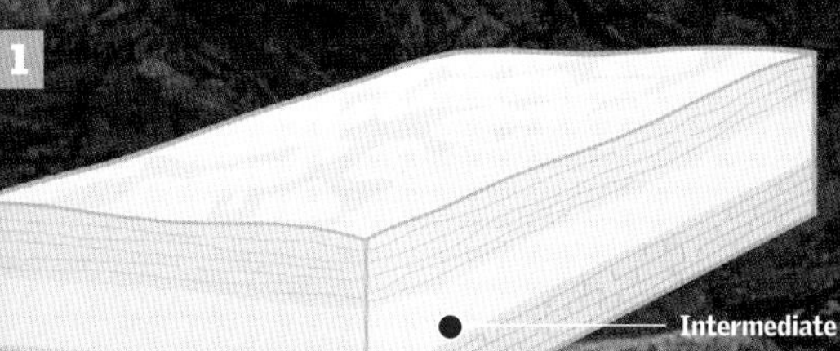

Contact Metamorphism

Magmatic rocks transmit heat, so a body of magma can heat rocks on contact. The affected area, located around an igneous intrusion or lava flow, is called an aureole. Its size depends on the intrusion and on the magma's temperature. The minerals of the surrounding rock turn into other minerals, and the rock metamorphoses.

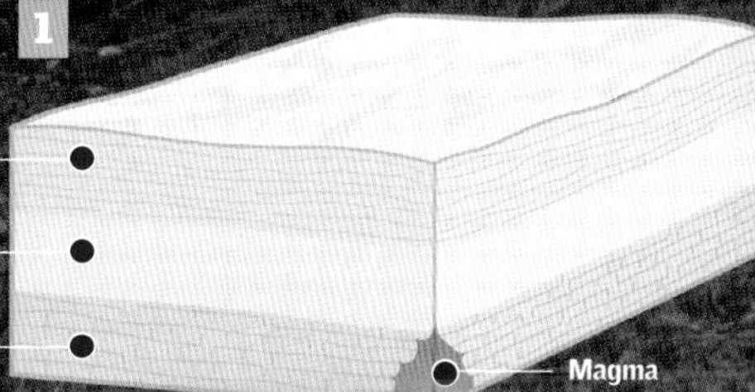

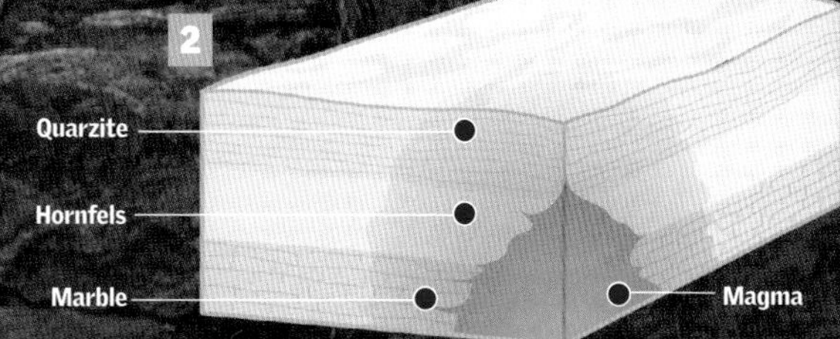

PRESSURE
As the pressure increases on the rocks, the mineralogical structure of rocks is reorganized, which reduces their size.

TEMPERATURE
The closer the rock is to the heat source and the greater the temperature, the higher the degree of metamorphism that takes place.

The Basis of Life

Organisms are born, live, reproduce, and die on a natural layer of soil. From this layer, crops are harvested, livestock are raised, and construction materials are obtained. It establishes the link between life and the mineral part of the planet. Through the action of climate and biological agents, soil forms where rocks are broken down. ●

300 years

The time needed for the natural formation of soil with its three basic layers, or horizons.

Types of Soil

In the soil we find bedrock materials that have been greatly altered by air and water, living organisms, and decomposed organic materials. The many physical and chemical transformations that it undergoes produce different types of soil, some richer in humus, other with more clay, and so on. The soil's basic texture depends to a great extent on the type of bedrock from which the soil is formed.

RANKER

develops on top of slightly altered bedrock. It is typical in high mountains, especially if it forms on granite or other acidic rocks.

0.2% of the world's land surface

PERMAFROST

Areas near the poles

The soil is saturated with frozen water. In the parts that thaw, big puddles are formed. Because of its characteristics, many animals cannot live there.

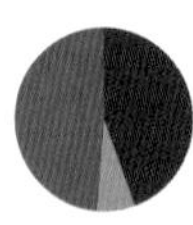

20% of the world's land surface

DESERTIC

Arid soil

Containing very little humus, it rests directly on mineral deposits and rock fragments.

14% of the world's land surface

LATERITE

Typical tropical soil

With abundant rains and humidity in these zones, the soil is well drained. The rain leaves a mix of oxides and hydroxides of aluminum, iron, manganese, nickel, and other minerals in the soil. This represents 70 percent of the world's iron reserves.

10% of the world's land surface

HOW IT FORMS

Much of the Earth's crust is covered with a layer of sediment and decomposing organic matter. This layer, called soil, covers everything except very steep slopes. Although it is created from decomposing plant and animal remains, the soil is a living and changing system. Its tiniest cavities, home to thousands of bacteria, algae, and fungi, are filled with water or air. These microorganisms speed up the decomposition process, turning the soil into a habitat favorable to plant roots as well as small animals and insects.

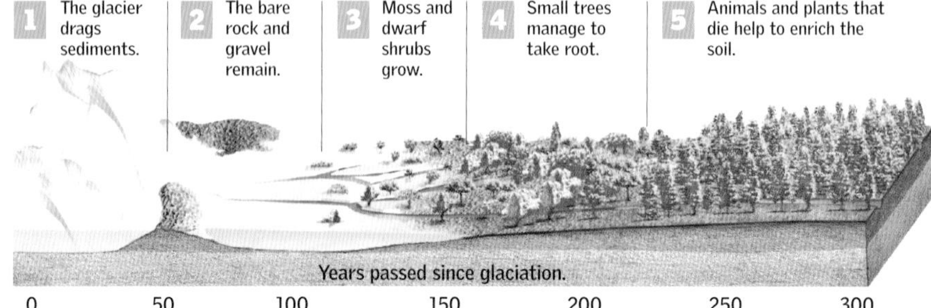

Different Characteristics

Observing the soil profile makes it possible to distinguish layers called horizons. Each layer has different characteristics and properties, hence the importance of identifying the layers to study and describe them. The surface layer is rich in organic matter. Beneath is the subsoil, where nutrients accumulate and some roots penetrate. Deeper down is a layer of rocks and pebbles.

0

UPPER LAYER
This layer is dark and rich in nutrients. It contains a network of plant roots along with humus, which is formed from plant and animal residues.

3 ft (1 m)

SUBSOIL
contains many mineral particles from the bedrock. It is formed by complex humus.

7 ft (2 m)

10 ft (3 m)

BEDROCK
The continuous breakdown and erosion of the bedrock helps increase the thickness of the soil. Soil texture also depends to a great extent on the type of bedrock on which it forms.

Living Organisms in the Soil

Many bacteria and fungi live in the soil; their biomass usually surpasses that of all animals living on the surface. Algae (mainly diatoms) also live closest to the surface, where there is most light. Mites, springtails, cochineal insects, insect larvae, earthworms, and others are also found there. Earthworms build tunnels that make the growth of roots easier. Their droppings retain water and contain important nutrients.

EARTHWORMS
It takes approximately 6,000 earthworms to produce 3,000 pounds (1,350 kg) of humus.

HUMUS
is the substance composed of organic materials, usually found in the upper layers of soil. It is produced by microorganisms, mainly acting on fallen branches and animal droppings. The dark color of this highly fertile layer comes from its high carbon content.

Rock Cycle

Some rocks go through the rock cycle to form soil. Under the action of erosive agents, rocks from the Earth's crust take on characteristic shapes. These shapes are a consequence partly of the rock's own composition and partly of several effects caused by erosive agents (meteorological and biological) responsible for breaking down rocky material.

Clouds of dust and ash are released to the atmosphere.

Ash and other pyroclastic materials are deposited in layers.

A volcano expels lava and pyroclastic material.

Igneous rock cools down and erodes.

EROSION

IGNEOUS ROCK
Extrusive rocks form as the lava cools.

Some sedimentary and metamorphic rocks erode, forming new strata.

These layers compress and harden.

Magma rises to the surface and comes out as lava through the volcano.

SEDIMENTARY ROCK

Igneous and plutonic rocks form as magma cools and solidifies below the Earth's surface.

Heat and pressure can recrystallize the rock without melting it, turning it into another type of rock.

METAMORPHIC ROCK

The rock melts to form magma.

If it is hot enough, the rock can turn into magma again.

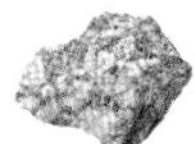

IGNEOUS ROCK

Divine and Worshiped

Formed millions of years ago, some rocks enjoy the privilege of being considered deities. Pagans, Christians, Muslims, and Aborigines of Australia base part of their beliefs on the myths, properties, or legends of a rock. Among the best known are Uluru (Ayers Rock), the Black Stone located in the cube-shaped sepulcher of the Ka`bah, and the rocks of Externsteine, a destination of Christian pilgrimages and a sacred site for many ancient pagan religions. Their origins are described and studied in theology as well as in geology. Resistant to the passing of time, they are transformed into myths that remain to the present.●

ULURU-KATA TJUTA NATIONAL PARK,
Australia

Latitude 25° S
Longitude 131° E

The great reddish rock of Uluru was created during the Alice Springs orogeny, 400 million years ago. The sandstone and conglomerates that formed the ancient alluvial fans folded and fractured deeply, turning horizontal layers on their ends.

100 feet (30 m)

the height of the Externsteine formation. It consists of five limestone pillars, riddled with caves, passages, and secret chambers.

Externsteine

Made of oddly twisted limestone rocks, Externsteine is located in the Teutoburg Forest north of the Rhine River in Rhineland, Germany. It was the place of heroic myths and German legends. It is also related to the Scandinavian Eddas and, during Nazism, to the Aryan myth. According to popular belief, the stones were placed there at night by giants; they were then burned by the devil, which explains their grotesque appearance.

Beliefs

Each crack, protuberance, or groove of a rock has meaning to Aborigines. For example, a rock's orifices symbolize the eyes of a dead enemy.

Uluru

Sacred place for Australian Aborigines for thousands of years, Uluru (Ayers Rock) is four miles (9.5 km) in circumference and rises 1,100 feet (340 m) above the Australian desert. Uluru was discovered by Caucasians in 1872 and renamed Ayers Rock in honor of the Australian Prime Minister Henry Ayers. In this enormous sandstone mass, dozens of dream paths traversed by the Aborigines and the paths already traveled by their ancestors in the past converge through a series of myths. In this manner, all the sacred places are connected. On the rock are forms such as Kuniya women and the wounded head of the Liru warrior, among others.

CAVE PAINTINGS

Uluru contains some of the most representative features of the ancestral history of the Aborigines. The caves surrounding the base of the rock have some Aboriginal paintings illustrating the paths and limits of the Dream Time. Many carvings in the caves are considered to be of divine origin.

MUSLIM TRADITION

Muslims who have the necessary means are expected to go to Mecca at least once in their lives.

The Black Stone of the Ka`bah

Located in one corner of the Ka`bah, the Black Stone is the most sacred treasure of the Islamic world. The Ka'bah is a cubic building located in Mecca, toward which Muslims face as they pray five times a day. The stone's exposed surface is 6 x 8 inches (16 x 20 cm), and its pieces are held together by a frame with a silver band. Muslims relate its origin to Adam and say that Abraham and his son Ishmael built the Ka`bah, but it was the Prophet Muhammad who converted Mecca into the sacred center of Islam in the 7th century.

Classes of Rocks

Different types of rocks can be distinguished based on their luster, density, and hardness, among other properties. A geode looks like a common rock on the outside, but when it is cut in half, a fantastic range of colors and shapes can be revealed. The several classes of rocks can also be grouped according to how they formed, giving us

BEAUTIFUL AND STRANGE
The inside of a geode, a rock filled with crystals, usually displays a beautiful formation.

HOW TO IDENTIFY ROCKS 62-63
IGNEOUS ROCKS 64-65
MARINE SEDIMENTS 66-67
COLLECTION OF DETRITAL ROCKS 68-69
ORGANIC ROCKS 70-71
COMMON METAMORPHIC ROCKS 72-73
INCREDIBLE PETRA 74-75

the categories of igneous, metamorphic, and sedimentary rocks. Most characteristics of rocks depend on their constituent minerals. There are also organic rocks, formed through the accumulation of the remains of organisms that decomposed millions of years ago. Coal and some types of carbonate and siliceous rocks are part of this group. ●

How to Identify Rocks

Rocks can be classified as igneous, metamorphic, or sedimentary according to the manner in which they were formed. Their specific characteristics depend on the minerals that constitute them. Based on this information, it is possible to know how rocks gained their color, texture, and crystalline structure. With a little experience and knowledge, people can learn to recognize and identify some of the rocks that they often see.

ANGULAR
Rocks have this shape when they have not been worn down.

Shapes

The final shape that a rock acquires depends to a great extent on its resistance to outside forces. The cooling process and subsequent erosion also influence the formation of rocks. Despite the changes caused by these processes, it is possible to infer information about a rock's history from its shape.

ROUNDED
The wear caused by erosion and transport gives rocks a smooth shape.

Age

Being able to accurately determine the age of a rock is very useful in the study of geology.

Mineral Composition

Rocks are natural combinations of two or more minerals. The properties of rocks will change in accordance with their mineralogical composition. For instance, granite contains quartz, feldspar, and mica; the absence of any of these elements would result in a different rock.

Color

The color of a rock is determined by the color of the minerals that compose it. Some colors are generated by the purity of the rock, whereas others are produced by the impurities present in it. Marble, for instance, can have different shades if it contains impurities.

WHITE
If the rock is a marble composed of pure calcite or dolomite, it is usually white.

BLACK
Various impurities give rise to different shades in the marble.

0.4 inch (1 cm)

Fracture

When a rock breaks, its surface displays fractures. If the fracture results in a flat surface breaking off, it is called exfoliation. Rocks usually break in locations where their mineral structure changes.

WHITE MARBLE
IMPURITY
WHITE MARBLE
PEGMATITE
WHITE MARBLE

Texture

refers to the size and arrangement of grains that form a rock. The grains can be thick, fine, or even imperceptible. There are also rocks, such as conglomerates, whose grains are formed by the fragments of other rocks. If the fragments are rounded, there is less compaction, and the rock is therefore more porous. In the case of sedimentary rocks in which the sedimentary cement prevails, the grain is finer.

0.4 inch (1 cm)

GRAIN
is the size of the individual parts of a rock, be they crystals and/or fragments of other rocks. A rock's grain can be thick or fine.

CRYSTALS
form when a melted rock cools and its chemical elements organize themselves. Minerals then take the shape of crystals.

Igneous Rocks

Formed from magma or lava, igneous rocks can be classified according to their composition. This classification specially takes into account: the relative proportion of silica, magnesium, and iron minerals found in these type of rocks; their grain size (which reveals how fast they cooled); and their color. Rocks that contain silica, along with much quartz and feldspar, tend to have pale colors; those with low silica content have dark colors created by iron and magnesium-containing minerals, such as olivine, pyroxene, and amphiboles. A rock's texture is determined by the configuration of its crystal grains. ●

Underground: Plutonic or Intrusive Rocks

Rocks of this type formed through the solidification of magma masses deep within other rocks. In general, they have undergone a slow cooling process in the Earth's crust, which has permitted the formation of pure mineral crystals large enough to be seen with the unaided eye. Usually they display a compact structure and have low porosity. Depending on the composition of the magma, there are acidic plutonic rocks (rich in silicon) or basic rocks (with low silicon content). Granite is the most common type of intrusive rock.

MACROPHOTOGRAPHY OF PINK GRANITE

GRANITE
This rock is formed by big grains of feldspar, quartz, and mica. Its light-colored components indicate an abundance of silicon and that the rock is acidic. Because of its great resistance to wear, granite is often used as a construction material.

GABBRO
This rock contains ferromagnesian minerals, such as olivine, pyroxene, and augite, which form dark-colored crystallizations, and feldspars, which give a white coloring to some of its parts. Gabbro generally solidifies slowly, leaving it with thick grains.

1 mile
(1.6 km)
THE MINIMUM DEPTH AT WHICH GRANITE FORMS

PERIDOTITE
This rock is mainly composed of olivine (which gives it a greenish color) and pyroxene. It is less than 45 percent silicon and is rich in magnesium, a very light metal. It is abundant in the upper layers of the mantle (at a depth of about 40 miles [60 km]) as a residue of old crust.

MACROPHOTOGRAPHY OF GRANODIORITE

GRANODIORITE
This rock is often confused with granite, but it is grayer since it contains larger numbers of quartz and sodic plagioclase crystals than it does feldspar. It has thick grains and contains dark crystals called nodules.

Dikes and Sills: Rocks Formed in Seams

Some types of igneous rocks are formed from ascending magma that solidifies in seams or fissures. The resulting sheetlike body of rock is called a dike if it has a vertical orientation or a sill if it has a horizontal orientation. The composition of these rocks is similar to those of intrusive and extrusive rocks. In fact, like dikes and sills, intrusive and extrusive rocks can also form in cracks. However, the manner in which the materials in a sill or dike solidify causes them to form crystalline structures different from those of their volcanic and plutonic relatives.

CRYSTAL JOINED BY VITREOUS MASS

PORPHYRITICS
These rocks solidify in two phases. In the first, slower phase, thick phenocrystals form. Then in the second phase, the phenocrystals are dragged along by magma, which causes the formation of smaller, vitreous crystals. The name porphyritic alludes to the color purple.

PEGMATITE IS NATURALLY SMOOTH.

PEGMATITE
This very abundant, acidic rock has a mineral composition identical to that of granite. However, its solidification process was very slow, thus enabling its crystals to grow to a size of several feet.

Index

PEGMATITE IS ASSOCIATED WITH THE PRESENCE OF GEMS AND RARE METALS.

Extrusive Rocks, Products of Volcanoes

Extrusive rocks form through the fast cooling of magma on or near the Earth's surface. Their structure and composition are closely related to the volcanic activity in the areas where they emerge. Because they are typically products of a fast solidification process, they usually have a very fine grain. When they are expelled from a volcano, they do not have a chance to crystallize before they cool, so they acquire a vitreous (glasslike) texture.

BASALT
This rock forms most of the oceanic crust. Its low silicon content gives it its characteristic dark color (between blue and black). Its rapid cooling and solidification gives it a very fine grain. Because of its hardness, it is used to build roads; it is not, however, used to make paving stones because it is too slippery.

PUMICE
This rock is produced from lava with a high silicon and gas content, which gives it a foamy texture. This explains its porous consistency—acquired during rapid solidification—which enables it to float in water.

OBSIDIAN
This rock is black; its shades vary in accordance with its impurities. Because it undergoes rapid cooling, its structure is vitreous, not crystalline; thus, it is commonly called volcanic glass. Strictly speaking, obsidian is a mineraloid. It was often used to make arrowheads.

GEOMETRIC PRISMS
These prisms were formed in the Giant's Causeway (Northern Ireland) through contraction, expansion, and rupture of basaltic lava flows that crystallized gradually.

Hexagon

THE MOST COMMON SHAPE INTO WHICH BASALT CRYSTALLIZES

Marine Sediments

Sedimentary rocks can also form through the accumulation and lithification of organic remains. The most common example is coral reefs, which develop underwater, surrounding the coasts of many temperate seas. Many limestone rocks also originate this way; they are made of calcium carbonate (calcite) or calcium and magnesium (dolomite). Because of their porous consistency, they often serve as repositories for fossil fuels, which are also of organic origin. Other rocks, like coquina, form through the accumulation of fragments of marine shells, lithified over time as materials filled and cemented their interstices.

68° F (20° C)

MINIMUM WATER TEMPERATURE NEEDED FOR THE FORMATION OF CORAL REEFS

FROM SEDIMENT TO ROCK

Under pressure from overlying layers, sediments are compacted and lithified, reducing their volume by 40 percent. Other substances dissolved in water (calcite, silica, and iron oxide) fill up the interstices between the particles of sediments, and when the water evaporates, cementation occurs.

COQUINA

CALCITE

CORALS IN ARIZONA

In the first phase of the Paleozoic Era (500 million years ago), the current mountainous region of the American West was a coastal area with much coral activity. This is how the abundant calcareous formations that can be seen today in Arizona's Grand Canyon originated. These formations also coexist with much younger rocks.

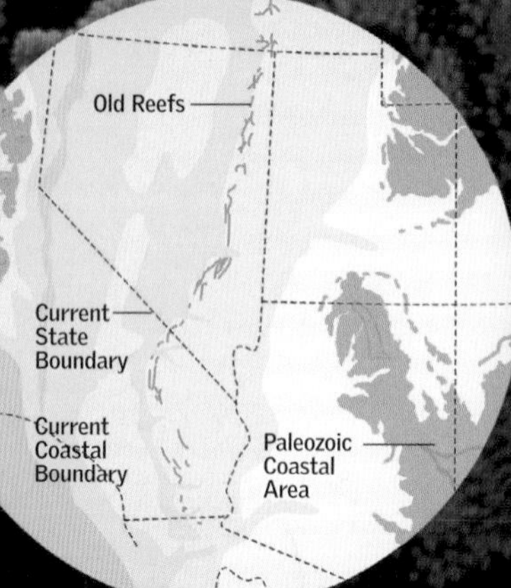

Coral Reefs

are rocky structures resistant to the action of waves and to the movement of the water. They are formed and/or colonized by photosynthetic organisms and marine animals, some of which have calcareous skeletons, as in the case of coral polyps. These soft organisms, related to anemones and jellyfish, live in colonies. When their solid calcareous skeletons sediment, they turn into calcite. They live in symbiosis with single-celled algae known as zooxanthellae.

FLAT CORAL
Corals typically grow in colonies and create reefs, layer by layer.

3 feet (1 m)
THE HEIGHT THAT A REEF CAN GROW TOWARD THE SURFACE IN ONE YEAR

Pearl, Jewel of the Sea

In order to protect themselves from the intrusion of a foreign body—such as a sand grain that becomes lodged between their mantle and shell—bivalve mollusks cover the intruding object with alternating concentric layers of protein (conchiolin) and calcite. This process ultimately yields a pearl. Fine pearls are produced by pearl oysters (Pinctada) in the warm, clear waters of tropical seas.

1 **LAYERS OF MOTHER-OF-PEARL**
Combination of calcite and a protein called conchiolin

2 **PEARL LUSTER**
results from the optical properties of crystallized mother-of-pearl.

Collection of Detrital Rocks

Among the sedimentary rocks, detrital rocks are the most abundant. They form through the agglomeration of rounded fragments (clasts) of older rocks. Depending on the size of the clasts, they are classified as (from smallest to largest) pelite, lutite and limestone, sandstone, and conglomerates. The analysis of their components, cementation matrix, and arrangement in layers makes it possible to reconstruct the geologic history both of the rocks and of the areas in which they are found. Some break off easily and are used in industrial processes and construction as rock granules, whereas others are appreciated for their toughness and hardness. ●

Clay, Lime, and Ash

These materials form the less porous, fine-grained detritic rocks. Lutites are rocks of clay, composed of particles whose diameter does not exceed 0.0002 inch (0.004 mm). In general, they are compacted and cemented through chemical precipitation. Limestone rocks are also called limolites, named after lime, a sedimentary material with a somewhat thicker grain (up to 0.0025 inch [0.06 mm]). Some rocks composed of volcanic ash have a similar granulation. These rocks are very important in construction.

COMPACTED ASH
It is possible to find one or more layers of fine-grained pyroclastic material (volcanic ash) in many sedimentary rocks. Rocks formed from larger pyroclasts, which solidified in the air during an eruption before they touched the ground, are rarer. Their origin is igneous, but their formation is sedimentary.

40%
THE REDUCTION IN THE VOLUME OF CLAY AS IT IS COMPACTED

TUFF
is rock that is formed from deposits of volcanic ash that has been cemented together. There are several types: crystalline tuff, which is largely composed of igneous glass; lithic tuff, which contains rock fragments; and hybrid tuff, which is formed from fragmented volcanic material combined with some clay.

CLAY (KAOLINITE)
When hydrated, it increases in size.

CLAY
The substance commonly known as clay is an unconsolidated rock, made of hydrated aluminum silicates and typically full of impurities. Kaolin is the name for pure granular clay; it is soft and white and keeps its color even after it has been fired in a kiln. It has scale-shaped microcrystals and generally contains impurities.

CHALK
Composed of calcite debris of biochemical origin, this mineral originates in the sea near the coast. After being eroded and transported, it accumulates on slopes where it becomes compacted. The chalk we use on blackboards is, in reality, gypsum.

COMPACTED
Very fine sediment

A Variety of Sandstones

Sandstone is rock composed of grains that are mostly between 0.003 and 0.08 inch (0.06 and 2 mm) in size. Sandstones are classified according to their mineral composition, their level of complexity (or geologic history), and the proportion of cementation material they contain. Quartzarenite (which is more than 95 percent quartz), arkose (which is mostly feldspar), red sandstone (which is cemented by iron compounds), and graywacke belong to this class of rocks.

SANDSTONE
is made up of small grains of sand that are here stratified by color and texture. This type of sandstone indicates that an alternating process of sedimentation involving two types of particles has occurred.

ARKOSE
possesses a varied composition, although it contains up to 25 percent quartz and feldspar. Generally, it has a porous consistency, and less than one percent of its interstices are empty. In this specimen, the pinkish section is composed of feldspar, and the white portion is quartz.

GRAYWACKE
has a defined proportion of calcium carbonate, quartz, feldspar, and mica. It differs from common sandstone because it contains a higher amount of cementation materials (more than 15 percent), which form its grain matrix. This makes it more compacted.

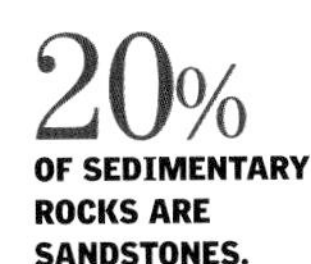

OF SEDIMENTARY ROCKS ARE SANDSTONES.

Conglomerates

Most of the grains that compose these rocks are larger than 0.08 inch (2 mm). In some cases, it is possible to identify with the unaided eye the primary rocks from which a conglomerate is formed. As a result, it is possible to determine the areas where the sediments originated. Accumulations of gravel and cementation material can indicate either slopes in the rocks where the conglomerates formed or the action of fluvial currents. All this information makes it possible to reconstruct the geologic history of a rock.

CONGLOMERATE
Formed by large fragments, they are good examples of sediments that have been compacted after landslides. The irregularity of this specimen's clasts points to a chaotic origin, which could be alluvial in nature or associated with a glacial moraine.

MICROPHOTOGRAPH OF BRECCIA

BRECCIA
Its grains are thick but with straight angles and edges. This shows that the sediments have not traveled far and that cementation has taken place near the area from which the materials originated.

85%
PERCENTAGE OF CLASTS LARGER THAN 0.08 INCH (2 MM)

Organic Rocks

Organic rocks are composed of the remains of living organisms that have undergone processes of decomposition and compaction millions of years ago. In these processes, the greater the depth and heat, the greater the caloric power and thermal transformation of the rock. The change experienced by these substances is called carbonization.

26%

OF THE PRIMARY ENERGY CONSUMED IN THE WORLD COMES FROM COAL.

Coal Formation

Plant materials, such as leaves, woods, barks, and spores, accumulated in marine or continental basins 285 million years ago. Submerged in water and protected from oxygen in the air, this material slowly became enriched with carbon through the action of anaerobic bacteria.

Transformation of Vegetation into Hard Coal

1. Vegetation

Organic compounds on the surface became covered by oxygen-poor water found in a peat bog, which effectively shielded them from oxidation.

2. Peat

Through partial putrefaction and carbonization in the acidic water of the peat bog, the organic matter changes into coal.

Contains 60% carbon

FORMATION OF PETROLEUM

In an anaerobic environment at a depth of about 1 mile (2 km), organic sediments that developed in environments with little oxygen turn into rocks that produce crude oil.

KEY

Gas

Petroleum (Oil)

Water

PETROLEUM TRAPS

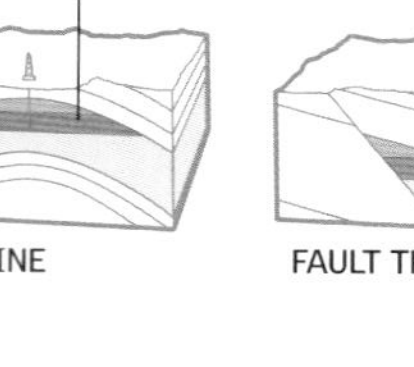

ANTICLINE

FAULT TRAP

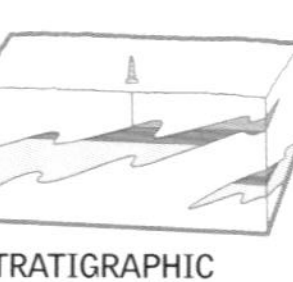

STRATIGRAPHIC TRAP

SALINE DOME

LOCATION INSIDE THE EARTH

Vegetation that will form peat after dying

The movements of the Earth's crust subjected the strata rich in organic remains to great pressure and transformed them into hard coal over the course of 300 million years.

SURROUNDING TEMPERATURE

Peat is compacted and transformed.

LEGEND

Exerted Pressure.

DEPTH

up to 1,000 feet (300 m)

TEMPERATURE

up to 77° F (25° C)

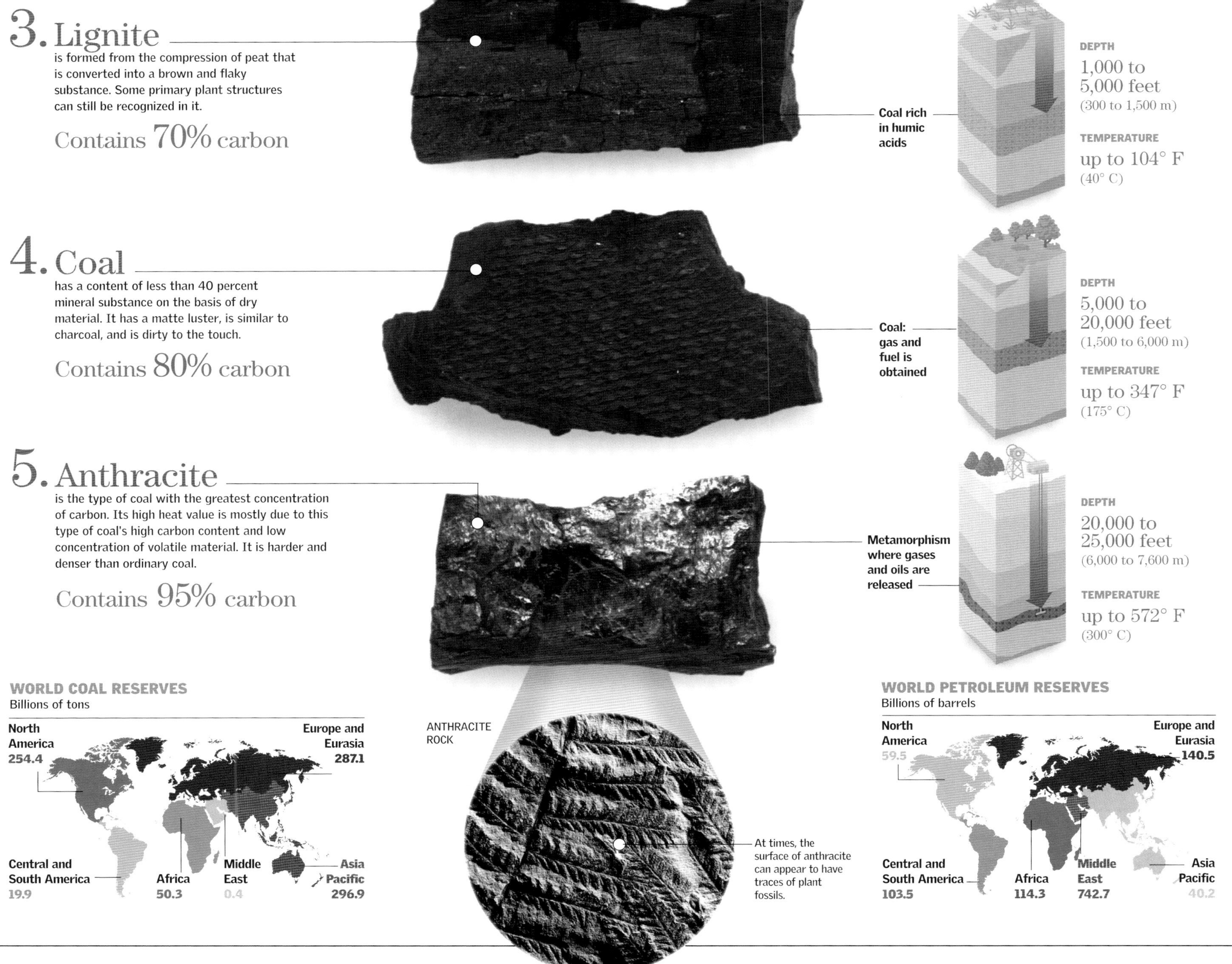
3. Lignite
is formed from the compression of peat that is converted into a brown and flaky substance. Some primary plant structures can still be recognized in it.
Contains 70% carbon
Coal rich in humic acids
DEPTH
1,000 to 5,000 feet
(300 to 1,500 m)
TEMPERATURE
up to 104° F
(40° C)
4. Coal
has a content of less than 40 percent mineral substance on the basis of dry material. It has a matte luster, is similar to charcoal, and is dirty to the touch.
Contains 80% carbon
Coal: gas and fuel is obtained
DEPTH
5,000 to 20,000 feet
(1,500 to 6,000 m)
TEMPERATURE
up to 347° F
(175° C)
5. Anthracite
is the type of coal with the greatest concentration of carbon. Its high heat value is mostly due to this type of coal's high carbon content and low concentration of volatile material. It is harder and denser than ordinary coal.
Contains 95% carbon
Metamorphism where gases and oils are released
DEPTH
20,000 to 25,000 feet
(6,000 to 7,600 m)
TEMPERATURE
up to 572° F
(300° C)
WORLD COAL RESERVES
Billions of tons
North America 254.4
Europe and Eurasia 287.1
Central and South America 19.9
Africa 50.3
Middle East 0.4
Asia Pacific 296.9
ANTHRACITE ROCK
At times, the surface of anthracite can appear to have traces of plant fossils.
WORLD PETROLEUM RESERVES
Billions of barrels
North America 59.5
Europe and Eurasia 140.5
Central and South America 103.5
Africa 114.3
Middle East 742.7
Asia Pacific 40.2

Common Metamorphic Rocks

The classification of metamorphic rocks is not simple because the same conditions of temperature and pressure do not always produce the same final rock. In the face of this difficulty, these rocks are divided into two large groups, taking into account that some exhibit foliation and others do not. During the transformation process, the density of rock increases, and recrystallization can induce the formation of bigger crystals. This process reorganizes the mineral grains, resulting in laminar or banded textures. Most rocks derive their color from the minerals of which they are composed, but their texture depends on more than just their composition. ●

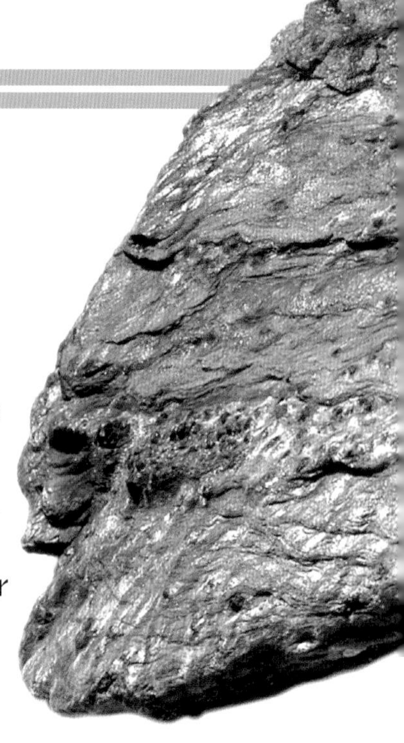

GARNETIFEROUS SCHIST
This rock's name comes from its components. Schist determines its texture and garnet its color and distinctive features.

SLATE MICROGRAPHY
Composed of foliated or laminated clay minerals

SLATE
Its black color comes from the carbon in organic matter present in sediments.

MICACEOUS SCHIST
Its characteristic coloring is determined by colorless or white muscovite crystals.

HORNBLENDE SCHIST
It contains some sodium as well as considerable amounts of iron and aluminum.

Slates and Phyllites

These foliated rocks recrystallized under moderate pressure and temperature conditions. Slate has very fine grains made of small mica crystals. It is very useful in the production of roof tiles, floor tiles, blackboards, and billiard tables. It almost always is formed through low-grade metamorphism in sediments and, less often, from volcanic ash. Phyllite represents a gradation in metamorphism between slate and schist; it is composed of very fine mica crystals, such as muscovite or chlorite.

PHYLLITE
Similar to slate, it is notable for its silky luster.

SLATE
Because of exfoliation, it tends to break into flat sheets.

Gneiss

Striped rock that usually contains long and granular minerals. The most common types are quartz, potash feldspar, and plagioclase. It can also have smaller amounts of muscovite, biotite, and hornblende. Its characteristic stripes are due to a segregation of light and dark silicates. Gneiss rock, which has a mineral composition similar to that of granite, is formed through sedimentary processes or derived from igneous rocks. However, it can also form through high-grade metamorphism of schists. It is the last rock of the metamorphic sequence.

Foliation

LAMINATED OR STRIPED TEXTURE, RESULTING FROM THE PRESSURE TO WHICH THE ROCK WAS SUBJECTED

Stripes

MAKE IT POSSIBLE TO DETERMINE THE DIRECTION IN WHICH PRESSURE WAS EXERTED ON THE ROCK.

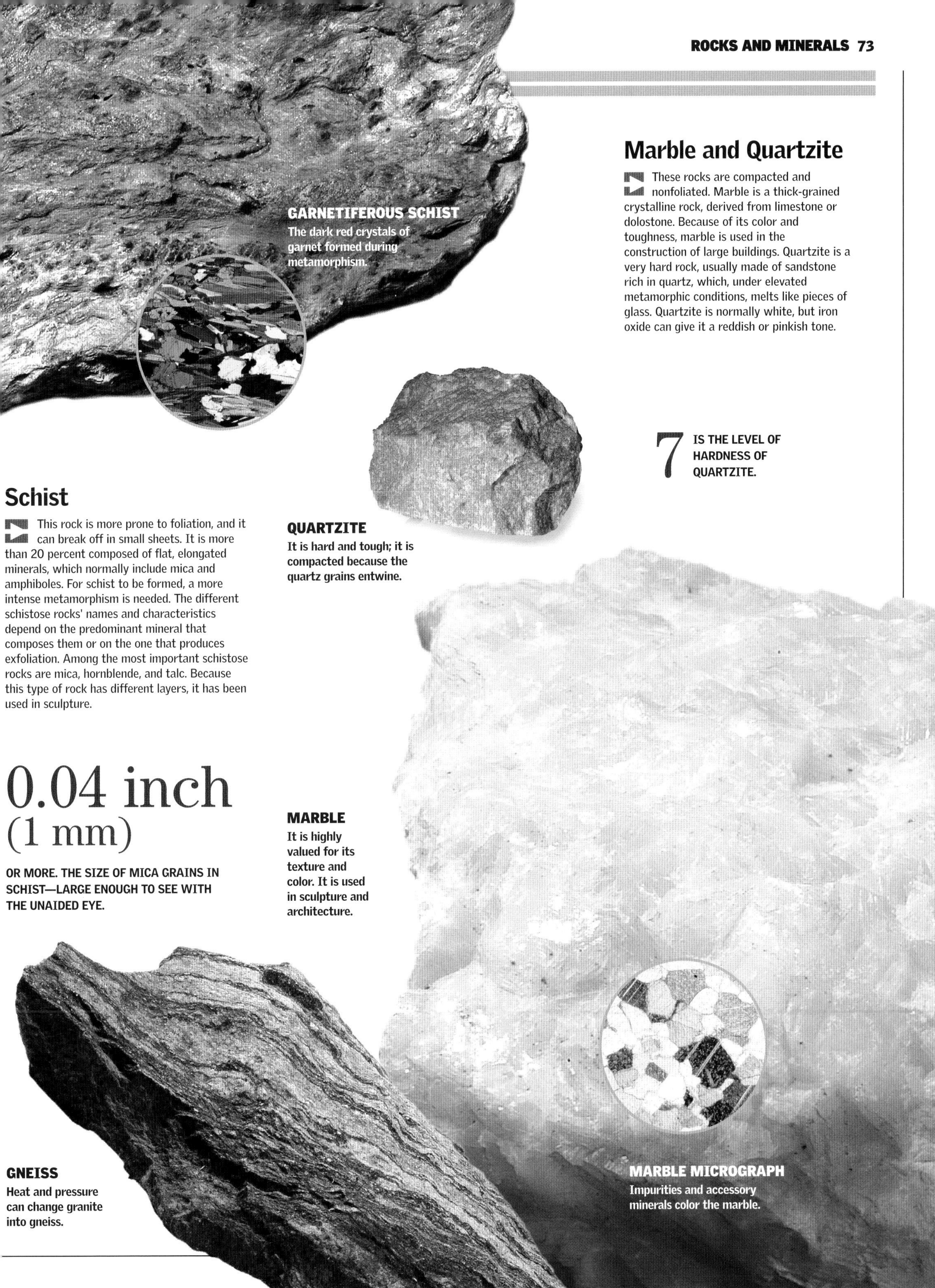

GARNETIFEROUS SCHIST
The dark red crystals of garnet formed during metamorphism.

Marble and Quartzite

These rocks are compacted and nonfoliated. Marble is a thick-grained crystalline rock, derived from limestone or dolostone. Because of its color and toughness, marble is used in the construction of large buildings. Quartzite is a very hard rock, usually made of sandstone rich in quartz, which, under elevated metamorphic conditions, melts like pieces of glass. Quartzite is normally white, but iron oxide can give it a reddish or pinkish tone.

7 IS THE LEVEL OF HARDNESS OF QUARTZITE.

QUARTZITE
It is hard and tough; it is compacted because the quartz grains entwine.

Schist

This rock is more prone to foliation, and it can break off in small sheets. It is more than 20 percent composed of flat, elongated minerals, which normally include mica and amphiboles. For schist to be formed, a more intense metamorphism is needed. The different schistose rocks' names and characteristics depend on the predominant mineral that composes them or on the one that produces exfoliation. Among the most important schistose rocks are mica, hornblende, and talc. Because this type of rock has different layers, it has been used in sculpture.

0.04 inch (1 mm)

OR MORE. THE SIZE OF MICA GRAINS IN SCHIST—LARGE ENOUGH TO SEE WITH THE UNAIDED EYE.

MARBLE
It is highly valued for its texture and color. It is used in sculpture and architecture.

MARBLE MICROGRAPH
Impurities and accessory minerals color the marble.

GNEISS
Heat and pressure can change granite into gneiss.

Incredible Petra

Historians from ancient Rome used to talk about a mysterious city of stone. In 1812 Johann Ludwig Burckhardt of Switzerland rediscovered it. Traces of Neolithic civilizations were found in Petra; however, its foundation in the 4th century BC is attributed to the Nabataeans, a nomadic people. The Nabataeans were merchants and raiders who became prosperous by controlling the spice trade. The city, carved in sandstone, knew times of splendor, but it eventually fell into ruin.

Temples and Tombs

The only way to reach Petra is by foot through a narrow passage among the rocks. The passage is 1 mile (1.5 km) long and, at some points, less than 3.3 feet (1 m) wide. The Treasury (Khasneh) is the first seen upon entering the city, followed by a Roman amphitheater. The buildings are carved into cliffs, and more than 3,000 old tombs have been excavated. The city also has fortifications.

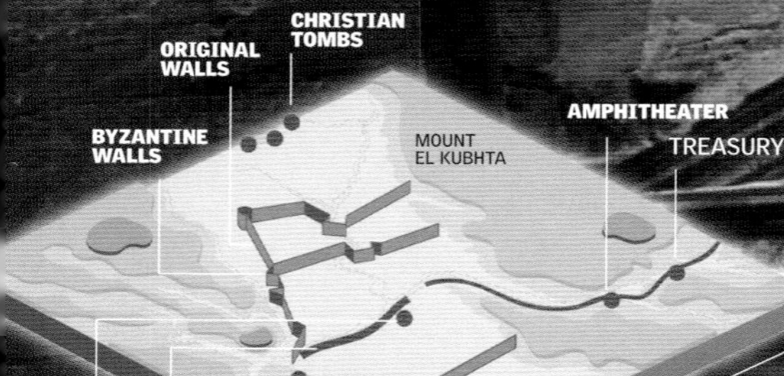

Tourist Attraction
The stone buildings were erected at different times over a period of 1,000 years.

HIDDEN IN THE DESERT
Petra is hidden in the mountains 155 miles (250 km) south of Amman, the capital of Jordan, and north of the Red Sea and the Great Rift Valley in Africa.

On the Rift

ITS CLIFFS ARE PART OF THIS FRACTURE; IN THE YEAR 363, IT WAS DAMAGED BY AN EARTHQUAKE.

Uncertain Origins

Petra's architecture is dominated by Greek, Egyptian, and Roman features; however, their symbiosis with Eastern elements is so great that to this day experts find it difficult to establish Petra's origin and dates of construction. The city's exterior adornments contrast with the interior sobriety of its temples. It contained sumptuous public baths that date from a time of splendor (1st century BC). However, most of Petra's population, which reached a peak of 20,000 inhabitants, lived in adobe houses.

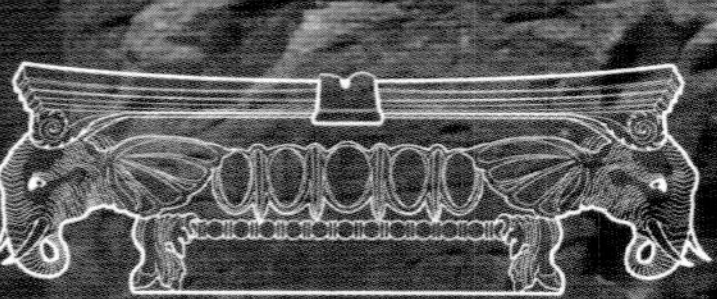

ELEPHANTS (Interpretation)
Native to Africa or India, elephants were not represented in classic culture. Here, however, they are seen adorning Greek-style capitals. This particular merging of cultures created expressions found nowhere else in the ancient world. Archaeologists find it difficult to date the pieces of art

The Treasury

IT WAS BELIEVED THAT THIS BUILDING HOUSED A PHARAOH'S TREASURE. ITS CUBE-SHAPED INTERIOR HAS SMOOTH WALLS AND IS LINED WITH MORTUARY CHAMBERS.

A Door Between Worlds

The statue represents the god Serapis, whose cult was established in the 4th century BC in both Greece and Egypt. Serapis is of Greek origin, but obelisks and cubic stones, typical Egyptian monuments, also abound in Petra. For a long time, it was believed that Petra was the biblical town of Edom. Its strategic location made it a transit area for Indians and Africans. The Roman and Byzantine empires had a profound influence: Petra was their gateway to the East. Beginning in the 7th century, though, Nabataean culture began to merge with Islamic culture, and it ultimately disappeared.

SERAPIS
God of prosperity and concealed mysteries. In Egyptian iconography, Serapis has horns.

CORINTHIAN CAPITAL (Interpretation)
One of the most classic capitals of Greek architecture, along with the Ionic and Doric styles

WINGED LIONS (Interpretation)
These carvings were located in the temple of Atargatis, goddess of fertility in the Nabataean culture.

Carved in Stone

The construction over sandstone respects and takes advantage of the characteristics of the landscape. To create openings, builders used the cracks and fissures that already existed in the rock. The sandstone in Petra is composed of at least two original types of sediments of different colors. Some people believe they are from different geologic phases, but it is more likely that the original sand was made of different grains.

SANDSTONE
A sedimentary rock with medium-sized grains (less than 0.08 inch [2 mm]), with great toughness and hardness. Its mineralogical composition can vary. In the Jordanian desert, it forms cliffs.

Use of Rocks and Minerals

Human beings have been extracting coal since ancient times, and mining generally takes place underground because most veins are hundreds of feet down. Human beings have to make incursions into the bowels of the Earth to extract its wealth. The materials extracted from the Earth are the basis of modern civilization, the raw

FOUND ALL OVER THE WORLD
Coal is found in almost all regions of the world, but today the only deposits of commercial importance are located in Europe, Asia, Australia, and the Americas.

IN DAILY LIFE 78-79
MOUNTAINS OF GOLD AND SILVER 80-81
AN OPEN-AIR MINE 82-83
BLINDED BY BRILLIANCE 84-85
BLACK AS COAL 86-87
BLACK GOLD 88-89
RADIOACTIVE MINERALS 90-91

material from which many products people use are made. Unfortunately, the Earth's reserves of coal, oil, and gas are being depleted. For this reason, other sources of energy to replace them are being sought. One of these alternative sources is nuclear energy. It requires uranium, an element found in certain rocks. ●

In Daily Life

It is impossible to conceive of modern life without the constant use of objects and materials made of rocks and minerals, metallic or nonmetallic. To illustrate this, it is enough simply to consider the elements that make up a car, trace them back to their origins, and consider the processes that shaped them. In some cases, the texture and characteristics of each material can be easily seen. Other materials, especially nonmetals such as coal and sulfur, are less noticeable, but they are a part of the production process as well. This process tends to emphasize and improve the physical, chemical, and electric characteristics of each material. ●

BODYWORK
Aluminum, titanium, magnesium, and steel

ALUMINUM
Light and durable

IRON
Strong and resistant

Hydrocarbons, the Source of Energy

The combustion of petroleum derivatives provides energy for propulsion. The combustion pathway begins with the storage of gas in the tank and ends with the expulsion of waste gases through the exhaust pipe. There a catalyst with thousands of cells filters the most toxic gases: carbon monoxide and nitrogen oxide.

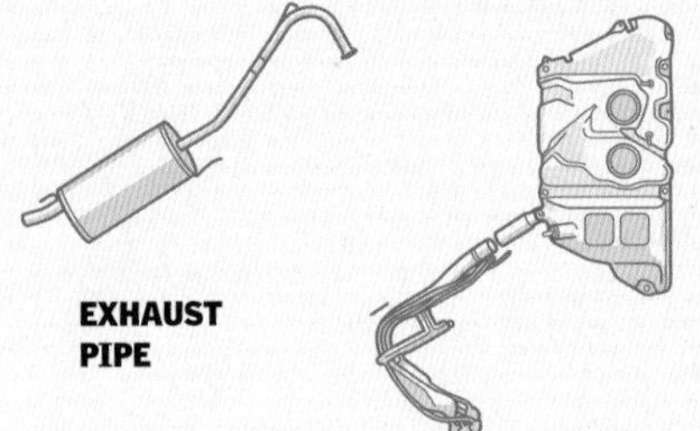

FUEL TANK

EXHAUST PIPE

Electric Properties: Conductors, Insulators, and Semiconductors

Metals, which tend to lose electrons, are the soul of electric cables and circuits. Nonmetals (and their polymeric derivatives) hinder the flow of electrons and are used as insulators. Other minerals, such as silicon, have intermediate properties: electronic components are manufactured by adding impurities to modify their properties.

CONTROL PANEL
In smaller contact areas, more expensive metals are used (gold is the best conductor). Chips and other electronic components contain silicon. Phosphorescent displays have strontium paint.

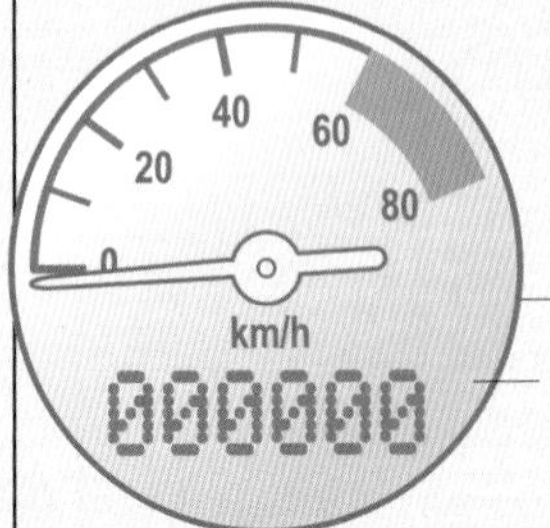

CIRCUITS
Gold, silver, palladium

DISPLAYS
Strontium

0.07 pound (0.03 kg)
PER CUBIC INCH
MAGNESIUM IS THE LIGHTEST METAL USED FOR INDUSTRIAL PURPOSES.

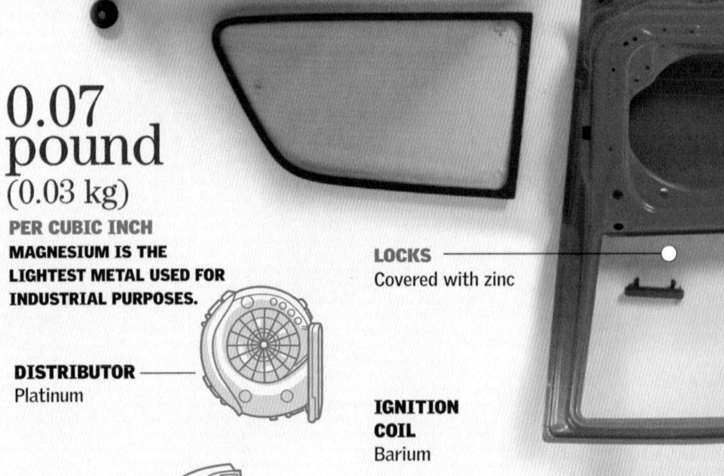

LOCKS
Covered with zinc

DISTRIBUTOR
Platinum

IGNITION COIL
Barium

HEADLIGHTS
Tungsten

Metals

The body of a car is made of iron (present in both steel and magnetite), aluminum, and magnesium. Other metals are used to produce parts that are resistant to torsion (vanadium, cadmium), temperature (cobalt), and corrosion (nickel and zinc). Barium and platinum are used in very specific parts, and other metals are used in smaller amounts in lubricants, fluids, or paints.

20%

MORE ALUMINUM IS REQUIRED BY VOLUME FOR THE SAME WEIGHT OF STEEL.

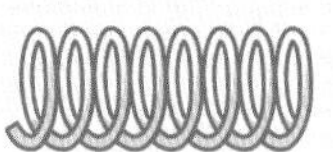

SPRINGS
Cadmium

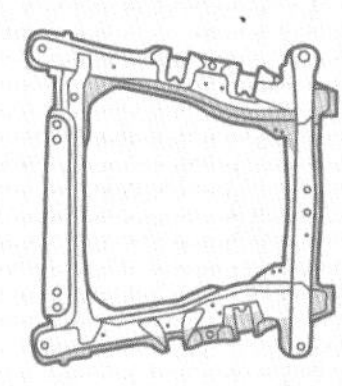

ENGINE BLOCK
It sustains the engine and is made of magnetite, an iron ore.

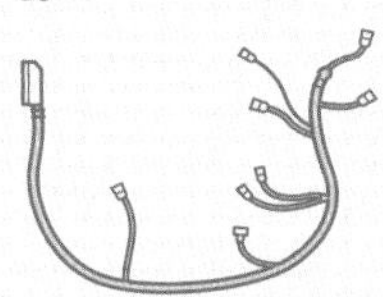

WIRING SYSTEM
Copper

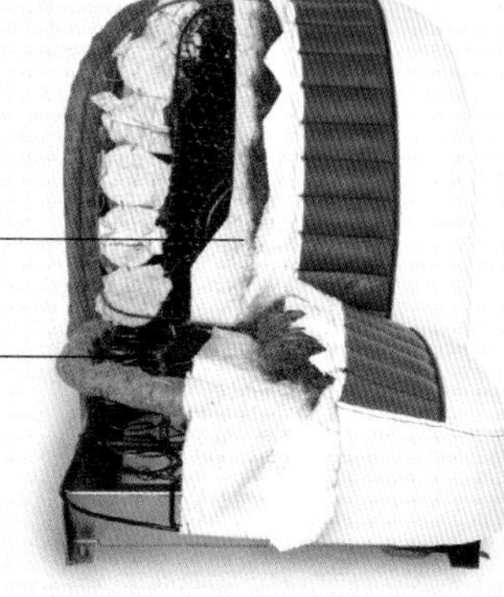

SEAT

BACK
Glass fiber

SPRINGS
Steel

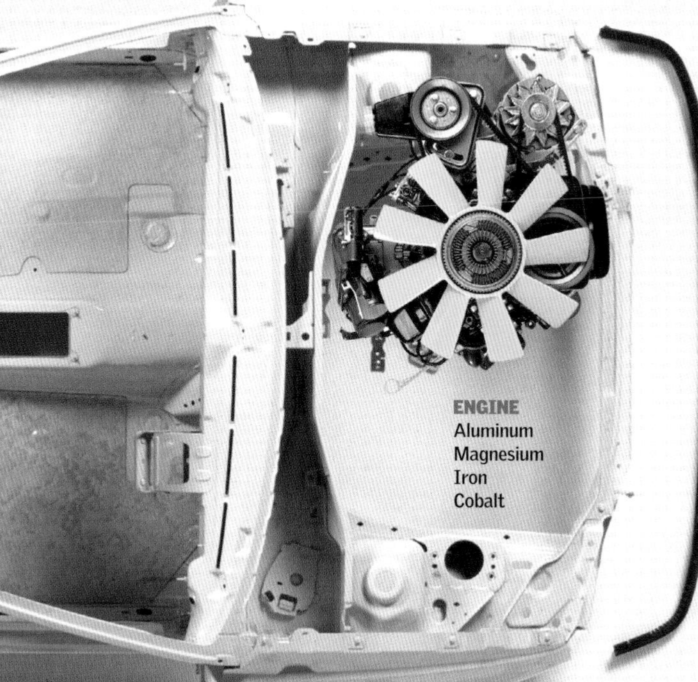

ENGINE
Aluminum
Magnesium
Iron
Cobalt

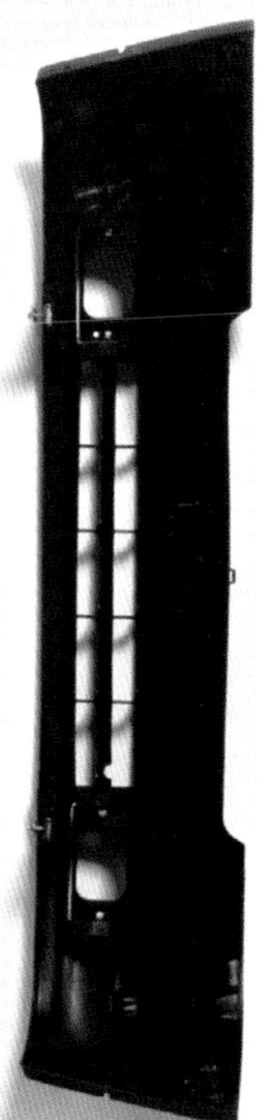

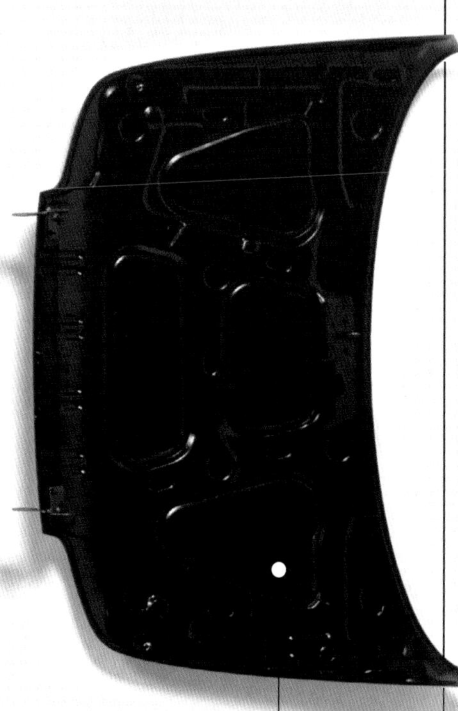

MAGNESIUM
Adds flexibility

MIRRORS
Glass and lead

WINDOWS
Glass (silica)

Nonmetals

Silicon and its derivatives (silicone, silica, and silicates such as asbestos) are omnipresent materials in car manufacturing. They appear in crystallized form, such as quartz, and in noncrystallized—or glass—form. Other nonmetals aid in the strengthening of metals—for example, carbon in the production of steel and sulfur in the vulcanization of rubber.

WHEELS
Titanium is often used in alloys and in the car's finish.

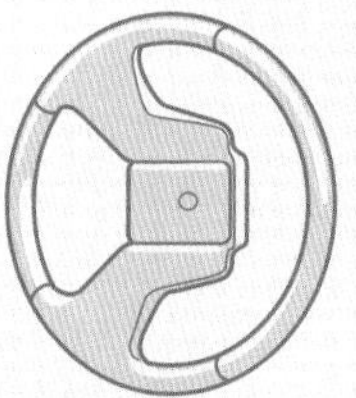

STEERING WHEEL
Silicon coating

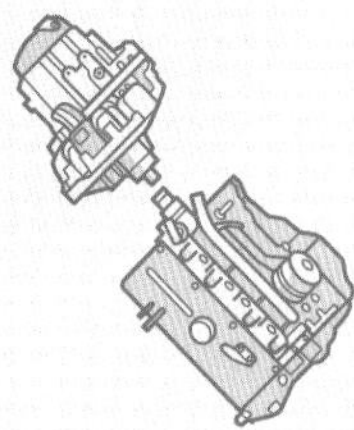

ENGINE JOINTS
Asbestos

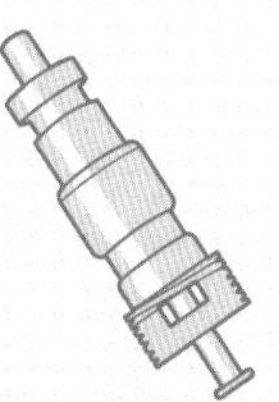

SPARK PLUGS
Porcelain (kaolin)

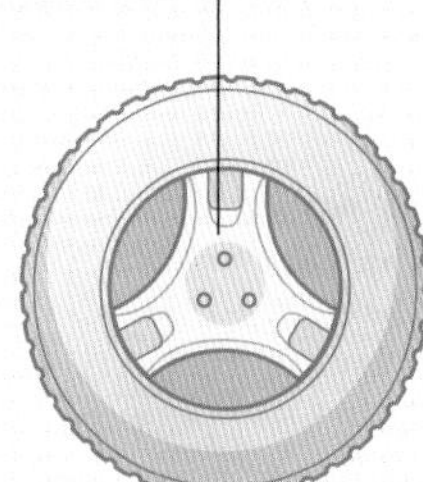

TIRES
Vulcanized steel mesh

Mountains of Gold and Silver

From the decision to exploit an area where valuable minerals are suspected to exist to obtaining these minerals in major amounts, large-scale mining operations require complex work that lasts for years. For instance, the exploitation of Veladero, an open-air gold-and-silver mine located in the province of San Juan in the Argentinean Andes and exploited by the Canadian company Barrick Gold, required more than a decade of research and development before the first ingots were obtained in October 2005. To reach the deposits, roads and housing were built for the workers. The potential environmental impact of the mine was analyzed since explosives had to be used and toxic substances, such as cyanide, were needed for extracting and separating the rock from other metals. ●

VELADERO, ARGENTINA

Latitude 29° S

Longitude 70° W

Total land area	1,158 square miles (3,000 sq km)
Employed builders (peak)	5,000
Gold reserves (1st estimate)	900 tons
Estimated life span	17 years

HUGE OPEN-AIR MINE

Veladero—located in the Argentinean province of San Juan, as shown on the map—required 2,300 tons of metallic structures and consumes 2,520 tons of sodium cyanide per year for extracting gold.

13,120 feet (4,000 m)

ABOVE SEA LEVEL
The elevation of the mine

1.

PROSPECTING
1 TO 3 YEARS
COST: $10 MILLION

Prospecting began in 1994. During this phase, the possible existence of a deposit covering a vast area was analyzed. It was necessary to draw maps, conduct studies, make satellite images, and undertake field trips to analyze superficial rocks.

NONPRODUCTIVE AREA
Areas that do not yield satisfactory mining results

FEASIBLE AREA
Opened by means of perforations and explosions

SUPERFICIAL ROCKS
During prospecting, field samples are collected for analysis.

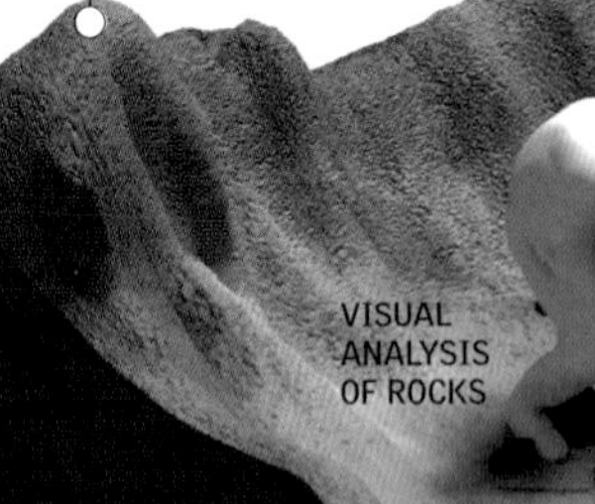

STRATA
Based on these features, geologic maps of the area are drawn.

DIRECT OBSERVATION
Geologists visit the area and take rock samples.

3. BLUEPRINT OF THE MINE

2 TO 5 YEARS

COST: $547 MILLION

Once the reserves and costs were analyzed, it was necessary to open the mineral deposit and evaluate the environmental impact of the operation. The infrastructure was then built; it included paths, houses, and river diversions.

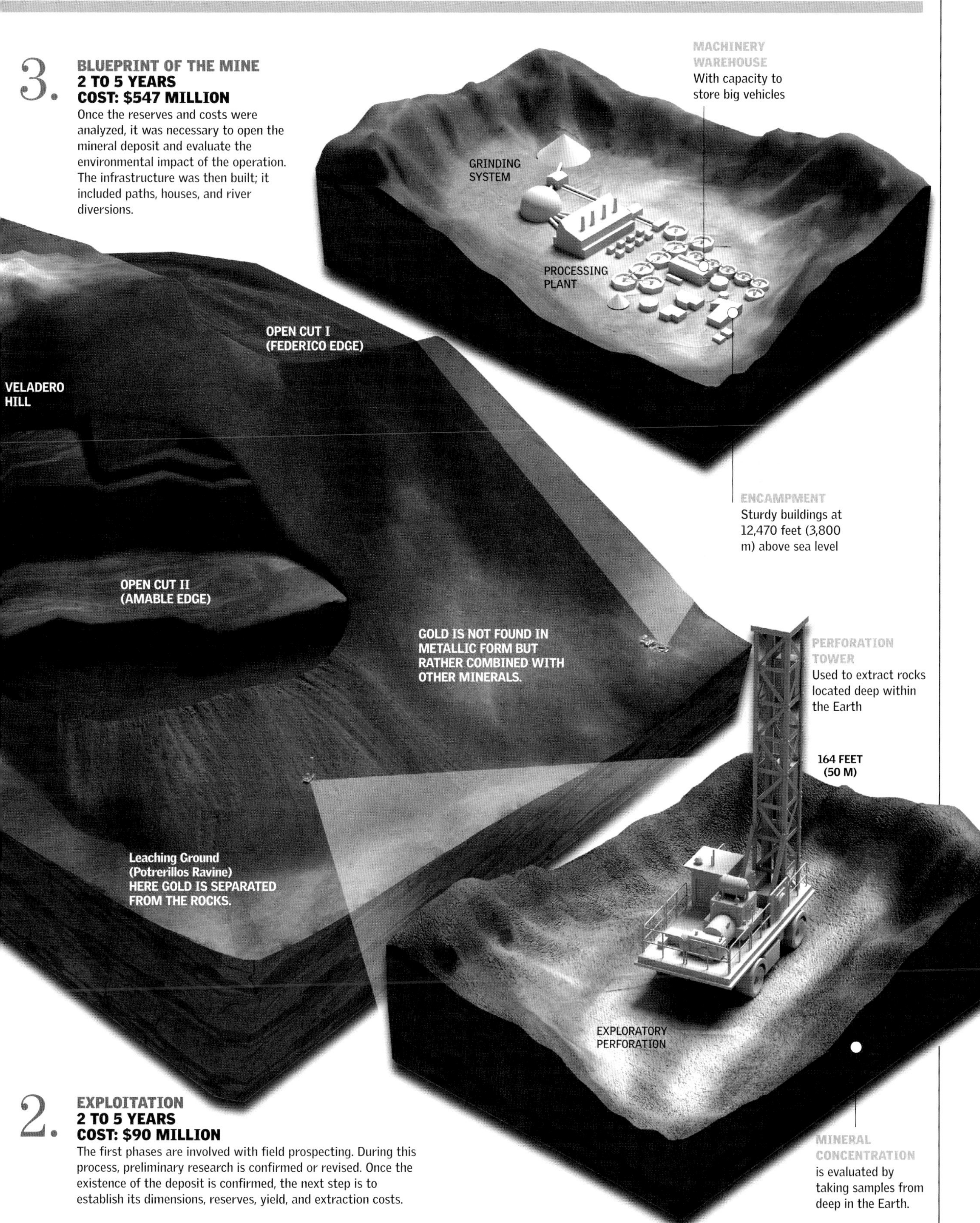

2. EXPLOITATION

2 TO 5 YEARS

COST: $90 MILLION

The first phases are involved with field prospecting. During this process, preliminary research is confirmed or revised. Once the existence of the deposit is confirmed, the next step is to establish its dimensions, reserves, yield, and extraction costs.

An Open-Air Mine

There are many types of mines. Some are located in the depths of the Earth, and some show their contents at its surface. Bingham Canyon, a copper mine located in Utah, is not only one of the most important open-air mines but also one of the largest excavations in the world. It is so large that it can be seen from space. It has been in operation since 1903, and it has been excavated in the form of terraces, like those used in agriculture. Its activity never stops, continuing even on weekends and holidays. The manner in which copper is extracted involves not only the use of machinery of extraordinary dimensions but also the use of a hydro-metallurgic chemical process called lixiviation, or leaching. Thanks to this process it is possible to obtain 99.9 percent of copper in its pure state from a copper concentration of 0.02 ounce per pound (0.56 gram per kg) of raw material.

How the Metal Is Extracted

Thousands of pounds of explosives, trucks and shovels as large as a house, and massive grinding machines that can reduce hard rocks to dust are involved in the extraction process, and rock temperatures are raised to 4,500° F (2,500° C). In this way, copper is extracted from one of the largest open-air mines on the planet. The raw material excavated from the terraces in the mine contains oxidized copper minerals. This material is transported to grinders, which produce rock fragments 1.5 inches (4 cm) in diameter. These materials are placed in a pile that is treated with a solution of water and sulfuric acid. This process is called lixiviation, or leaching. Lixiviation is a hydro-metallurgic treatment that makes it possible to obtain copper present in the oxidized minerals. The treated material begins the process of sulfatation of copper contained in the oxidized minerals.

HOW MATERIAL IS OBTAINED

The process begins with rock perforation and blasting. The rock is removed from the pit and loaded by large shovels onto trucks. Then it is unloaded onto a mobile grinder. The ground rock is removed from the mine on conveyor belts and then sprayed with a solution of water and sulfuric acid.

0.56 %

COPPER CONCENTRATION IN THE RAW MATERIAL

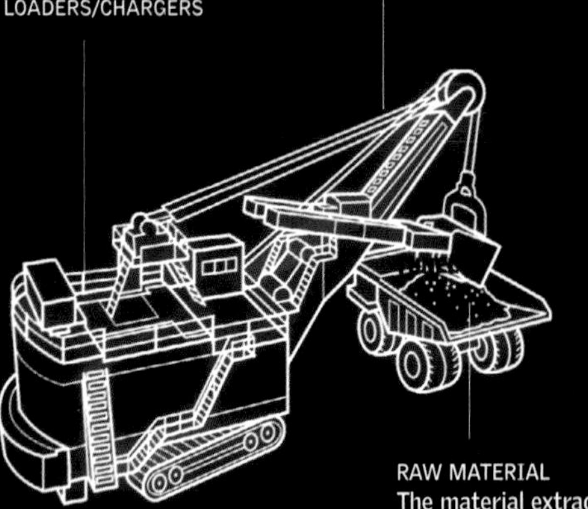

The material extracted from the pit is loaded on a mobile grinder.

2

ARRANGEMENT OF THE STACK

When on the conveyor belts, the material is taken to a place where it will form a lixiviation pile or stack, and a trickle irrigation system is installed on top of this pile. Sprinklers cover the entire exposed area. The material will spend 45 days here.

6 ounces/gallon (45 g/l)

OF COPPER IN THE SOLUTION AT THE END OF THE LIXIVIATION PROCESS

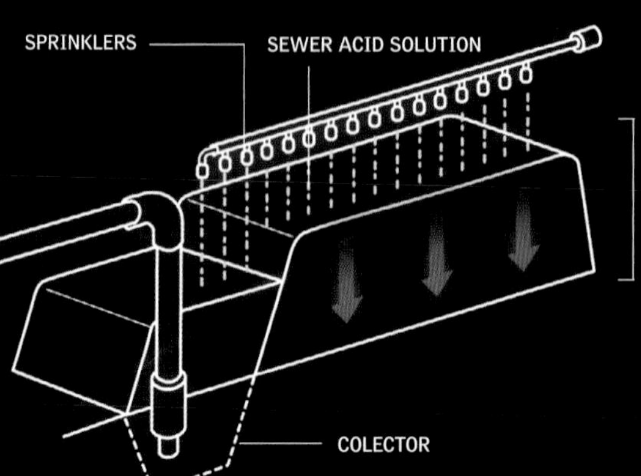

26 FEET (8 M)

LIXIVIATION

The hydro-metallurgic process that makes it possible to obtain copper from the oxidized minerals by applying a solution of sulfuric acid and water. Oxidized minerals are sensitive to attack by acid solutions.

BINGHAM CANYON UNITED STATES

Latitude 40° 32´ N

Longitude 112° 9´ W

Diameter of the pit	2.5 miles (4 km)
Depth of the pit	2,300 feet (700 m)
Opening year	1903
Closing year	2013
Number of employees	1,700

WATER BASIN
The phreatic layer, the closest aquifer to the surface below the water table, emerges at the bottom and forms a water basin with a peculiar color because of the copper salts in the deposit.

TERRACING OF THE SURFACE
The mine acquires a steplike shape because it is excavated in spiral terraces. The machines can move easily over the terraces, collecting the extracted material.

PATHS
The roads are well built, and they can withstand loads of up to 1,765 cubic feet (50 cu m) of rock on only one truck.

3 COPPER RECOVERY

The resulting copper solution is collected in conduits and then undergoes a process of electrolytic refining. During this process, electricity passes between two copper plates suspended in the solution; copper from the solution adheres to the sheets as it is separated through electrolysis.

99.9 %

COPPER IN A PURE STATE

COPPER SHEETS

ELECTROLYTIC POOL

TERRACES

BOTTOM OF THE MINE

MAXIMUM PHREATIC LEVEL

0.4 MILE (0.7 KM)

2.5 MILES (4 KM)

FORMATION OF THE MINE

Surface mines take the shape of large terraced pits, which grow ever deeper and wider. Viewed from above, an enormous spiraling hollow can be seen. This is a relatively inexpensive and simple method to extract high-purity materials.

Blinded by Brilliance

The discovery of gold in the Sacramento River in California in the mid-19th century started one of the largest migrations of its time. Fortune hunters came from the Americas as well as from Asia, but few were able to achieve their goal of striking it rich. Each year, obtaining gold required a larger investment of time and equipment, and equipment suppliers were the ones who ultimately earned the highest profits. Gold was the key force in settling California, now the wealthiest state in the United States. At its peak, immigration overwhelmed the state's social and municipal services as up to 30 houses were being built each day. ●

ENCAMPMENTS
Bad living conditions led to the death of many workers; many were also killed by epidemics and illnesses.

RÍO SACRAMENTO

DRAGGING
Mules dragged large stones, used to break other quartz stones, thus releasing the gold within.

WASHED PARTICLES

WASHING CONTAINERS

PARTICLES BEING WASHED

PAN
The swirling movement of the pan allowed for the separation of sediments, and the gold could be identified by a difference in weight.

CHINESE
Chinese immigrants, attracted by the prospect of wealth, constituted most of the labor force.

BY HAND
Resources and tools were scarce. Almost everything was done by hand.

1 **1848**
On the morning of January 24, while James Marshall was building a sawmill for his employer John Sutter, he discovered gold on the banks of the Sacramento River. This irrevocably changed the history of California.

$16
WAS THE PRICE OF A PLOT OF LAND; 18 MONTHS LATER, IT WAS PRICED AT $45,000.

1850
California became the 31st state of the Union. Slavery was abolished because of the large influx of immigrants and the fear that it would reduce workers' salaries. However, the Fugitive Slave Act was sanctioned by the state. According to this law, every fugitive slave that entered California had to be returned to his or her owner.

FLOW OF IMMIGRANTS

In 1848, California had a population of 14,000. However, within four years and with the gold fever at its peak, the population rose to 223,856.

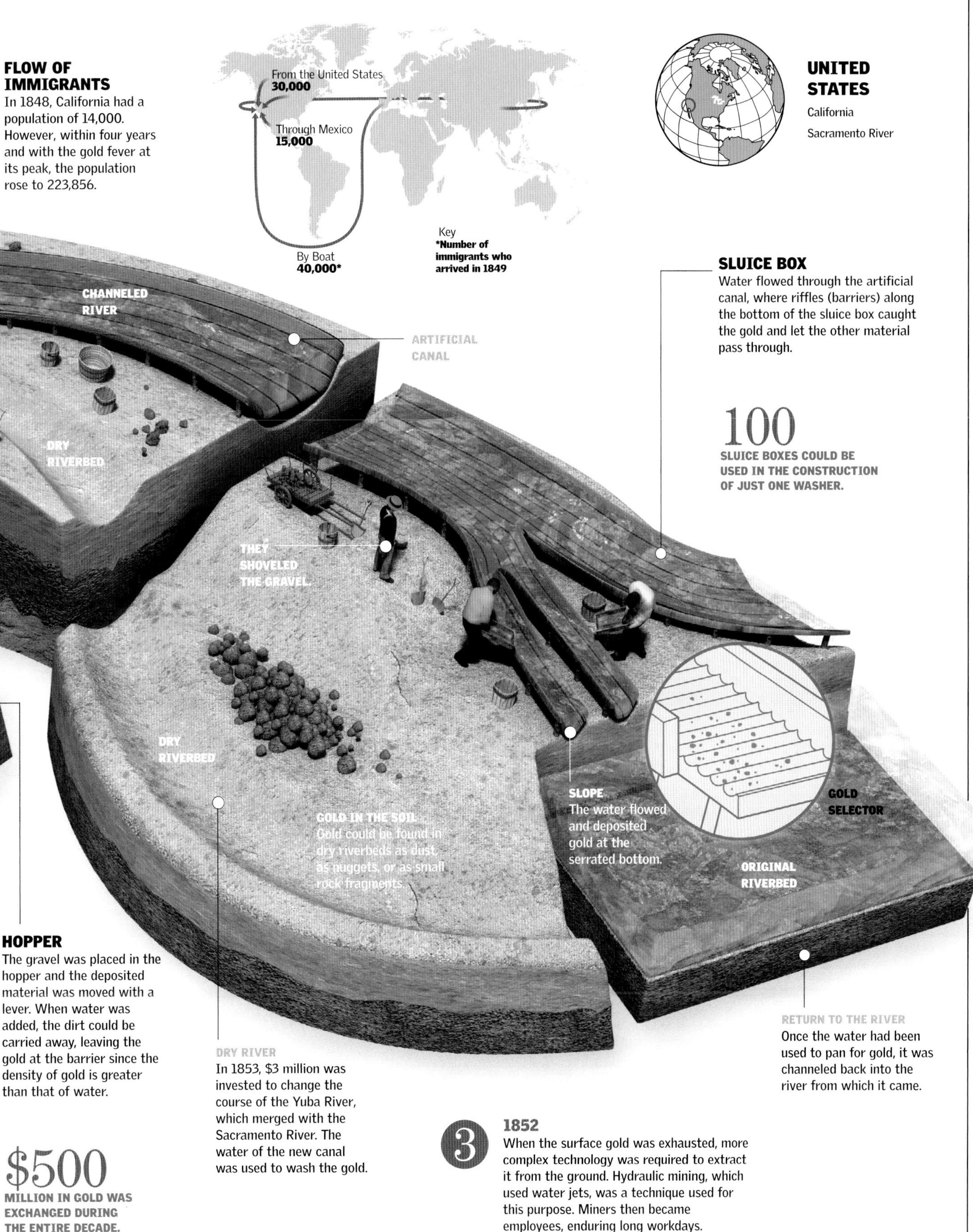

SLUICE BOX

Water flowed through the artificial canal, where riffles (barriers) along the bottom of the sluice box caught the gold and let the other material pass through.

100

SLUICE BOXES COULD BE USED IN THE CONSTRUCTION OF JUST ONE WASHER.

HOPPER

The gravel was placed in the hopper and the deposited material was moved with a lever. When water was added, the dirt could be carried away, leaving the gold at the barrier since the density of gold is greater than that of water.

DRY RIVER

In 1853, $3 million was invested to change the course of the Yuba River, which merged with the Sacramento River. The water of the new canal was used to wash the gold.

RETURN TO THE RIVER

Once the water had been used to pan for gold, it was channeled back into the river from which it came.

$500

MILLION IN GOLD WAS EXCHANGED DURING THE ENTIRE DECADE.

3 1852

When the surface gold was exhausted, more complex technology was required to extract it from the ground. Hydraulic mining, which used water jets, was a technique used for this purpose. Miners then became employees, enduring long workdays.

Black as Coal

In gallery or subterranean mines people must enter the bowels of the Earth to be able to extract the planet's mineral wealth. Some mines for extracting coal—the legendary driving force of the Industrial Revolution—are a clear example of this type of exploitation. Although these mines imply higher costs and labor risks, they have a lower environmental impact.

How Coal Is Extracted

6. DISTRIBUTION
Mine trains transport the coal from the mine to the point of consumption.

5. WASHING AND CLASSIFICATION
Coal that leaves the mine is mixed with mud and rocks. It must be washed and classified according to quality and size.

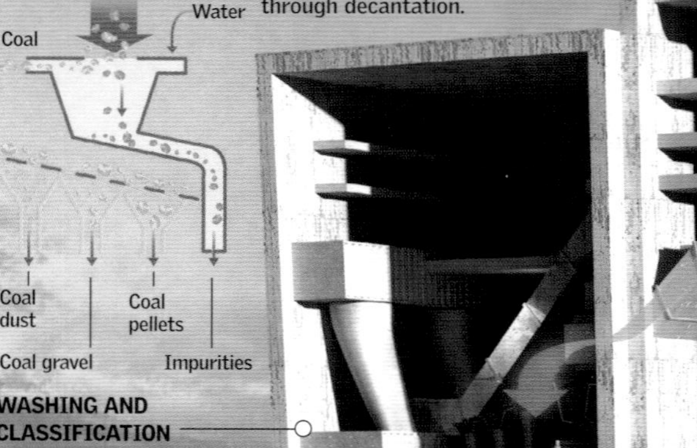

EXTRACTION TOWER

VENTILATION
Without good ventilation, methane, an explosive gas, condenses in the galleries and creates the risk of explosions.

60% OF EXPLOITATION IS CARRIED OUT UNDERGROUND.

MAIN PRODUCERS
Year 2003. In millions of tons.

China	1,635
United States	1,070
India	503
Russia	294
South Africa	264

MAIN CONSUMERS
Year 2003. In millions of tons.

China	1,531
United States	1,094
India	430
Germany	273
South Africa	264

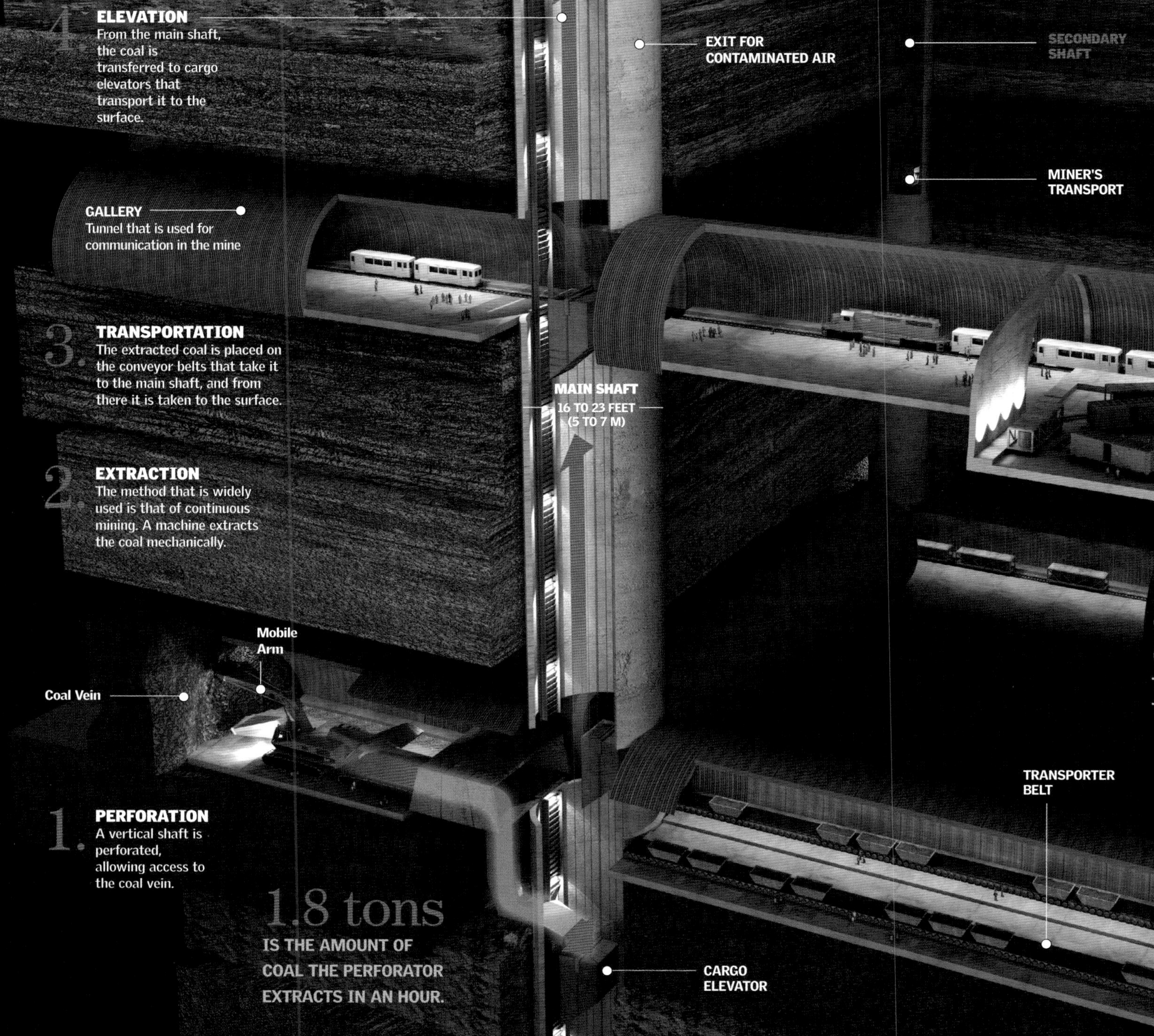
4. ELEVATION
From the main shaft, the coal is transferred to cargo elevators that transport it to the surface.
GALLERY
Tunnel that is used for communication in the mine
3. TRANSPORTATION
The extracted coal is placed on the conveyor belts that take it to the main shaft, and from there it is taken to the surface.
2. EXTRACTION
The method that is widely used is that of continuous mining. A machine extracts the coal mechanically.
Mobile Arm
Coal Vein
1. PERFORATION
A vertical shaft is perforated, allowing access to the coal vein.
1.8 tons
IS THE AMOUNT OF COAL THE PERFORATOR EXTRACTS IN AN HOUR.
MAIN SHAFT
16 TO 23 FEET (5 TO 7 M)
EXIT FOR CONTAMINATED AIR
SECONDARY SHAFT
MINER'S TRANSPORT
MOVEMENT IN THE GALLERIES
The miners travel on foot or by train to the coal vein.
5,000 feet (1.52 km)
THE SHAFTS CAN REACH THIS DEPTH.
TRANSPORTER BELT
CARGO ELEVATOR

Black Gold

Because of its economic importance as a source of energy, petroleum, or oil, is called black gold. Searching for it requires large amounts of money and years of investigation and exploration, all with no guarantees. Once discovered, petroleum extraction entails the use of expensive machinery, which includes everything from oil pumps to refineries that convert oil into many derivative products. The oil trade is one of the most lucrative businesses worldwide, and a change in its price can affect national economies and put whole countries on guard. Petroleum is a nonrenewable source of energy.

How Petroleum Is Obtained

1. SEARCH
Indirect methods are used to detect the presence of hydrocarbons. However, the information obtained is not conclusive.

2. EXPLORATION
Once a deposit is detected, the soil is drilled to verify that there is petroleum with economic potential.

3. EXTRACTION
If the well is productive, the drilling towers are removed and extraction systems are installed.

NATURAL WAYS TO PUMP PETROLEUM

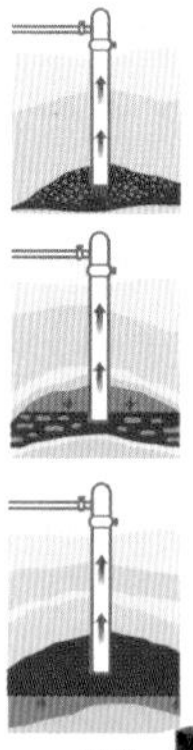

The driving force is the gas dissolved in a petroleum deposit.

The gas accumulated in the deposit pushes the petroleum outward.

Later as water is pumped in, it accumulates underneath the petroleum and pushes it upward.

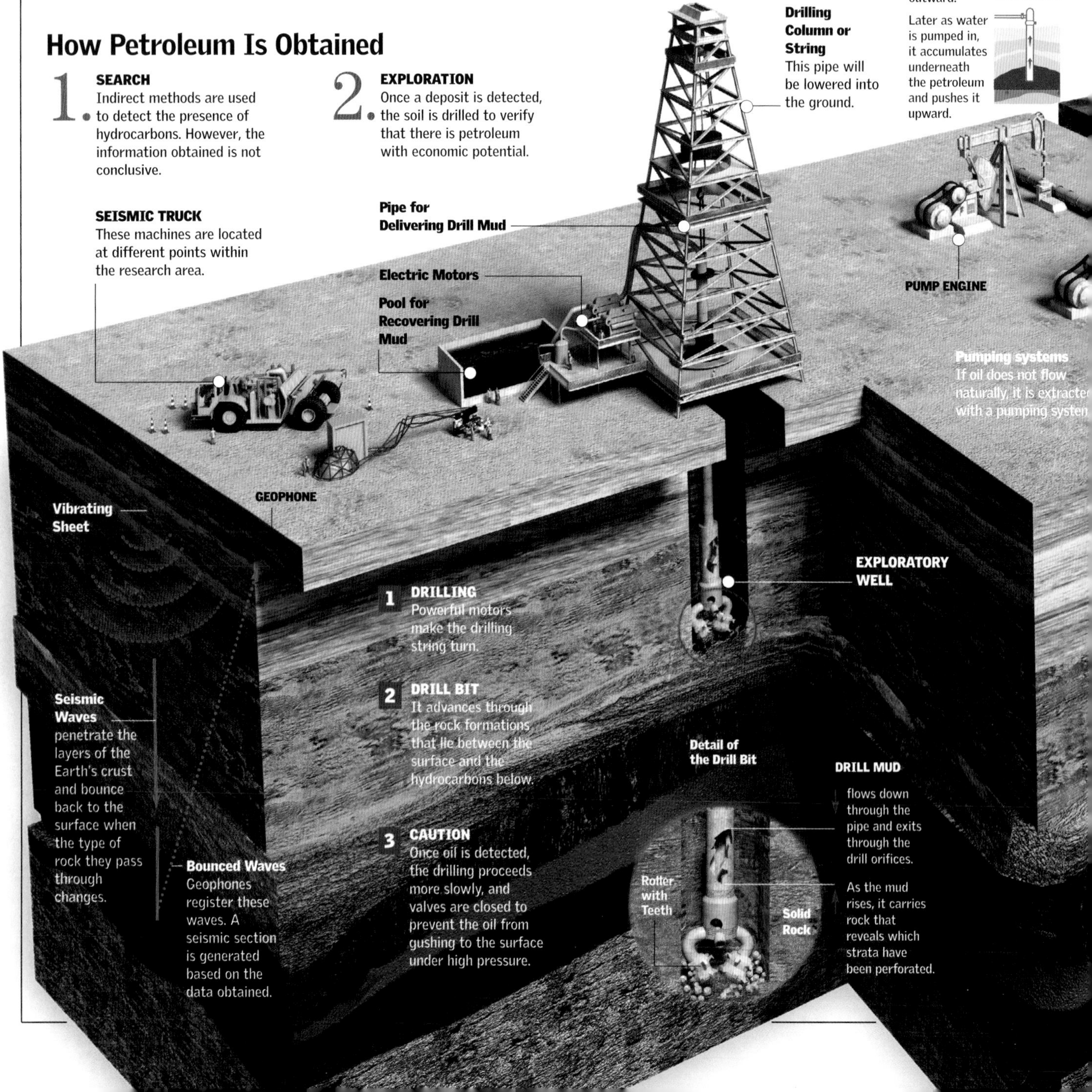

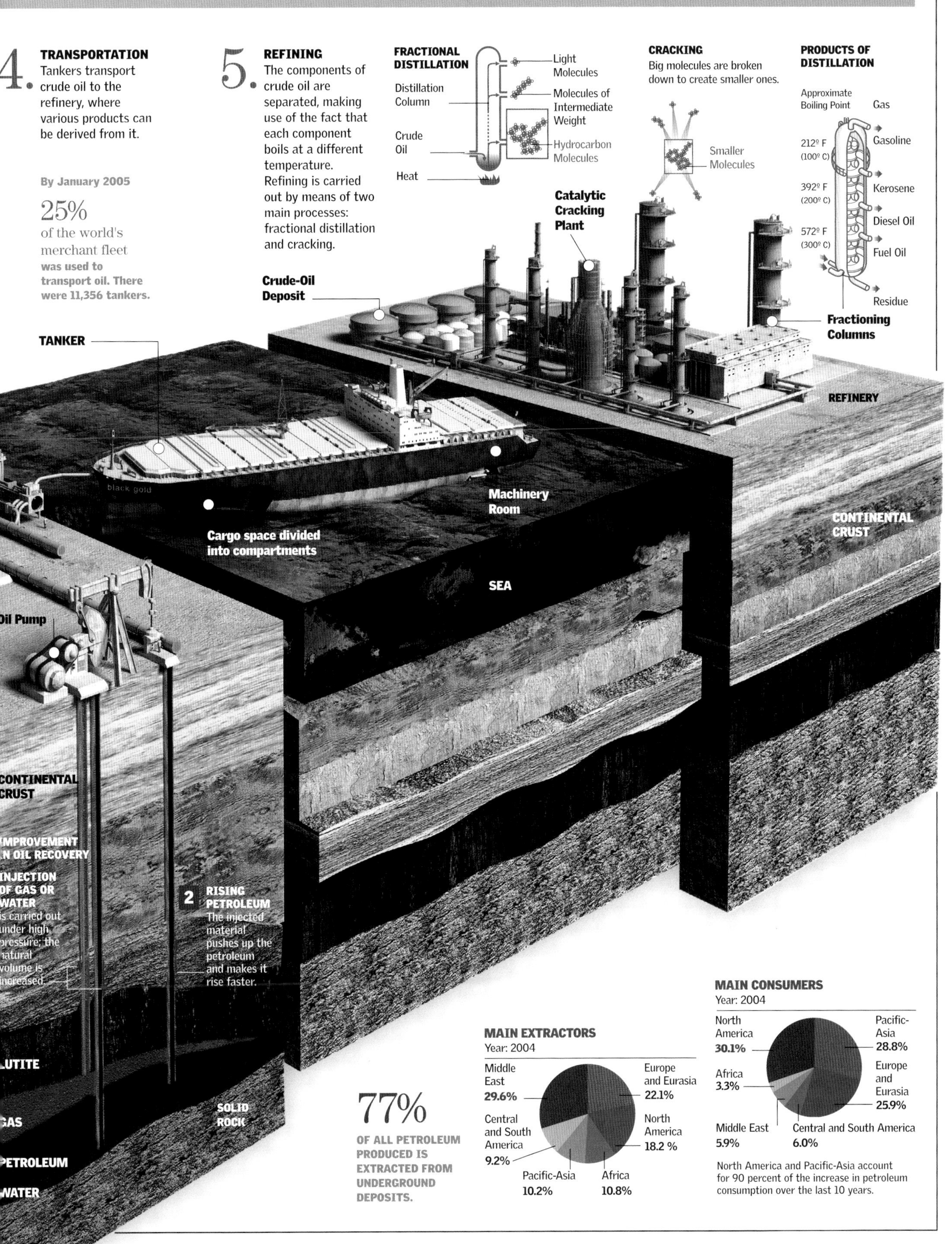

4. TRANSPORTATION
Tankers transport crude oil to the refinery, where various products can be derived from it.
By January 2005
25%
of the world's merchant fleet
was used to transport oil. There were 11,356 tankers.
5. REFINING
The components of crude oil are separated, making use of the fact that each component boils at a different temperature. Refining is carried out by means of two main processes: fractional distillation and cracking.
FRACTIONAL DISTILLATION
Distillation Column
Crude Oil
Heat
Light Molecules
Molecules of Intermediate Weight
Hydrocarbon Molecules
CRACKING
Big molecules are broken down to create smaller ones.
Smaller Molecules
PRODUCTS OF DISTILLATION
Approximate Boiling Point
Gas
212º F (100º C)
Gasoline
392º F (200º C)
Kerosene
Diesel Oil
572º F (300º C)
Fuel Oil
Residue
Fractioning Columns
Catalytic Cracking Plant
Crude-Oil Deposit
TANKER
REFINERY
black gold
Machinery Room
Cargo space divided into compartments
CONTINENTAL CRUST
SEA
Oil Pump
CONTINENTAL CRUST
IMPROVEMENT IN OIL RECOVERY
INJECTION OF GAS OR WATER
is carried out under high pressure; the natural volume is increased.
2 RISING PETROLEUM
The injected material pushes up the petroleum and makes it rise faster.
UTITE
SOLID ROCK
GAS
PETROLEUM
WATER
77%
OF ALL PETROLEUM PRODUCED IS EXTRACTED FROM UNDERGROUND DEPOSITS.
MAIN EXTRACTORS
Year: 2004
Middle East 29.6%
Europe and Eurasia 22.1%
North America 18.2 %
Africa 10.8%
Pacific-Asia 10.2%
Central and South America 9.2%
MAIN CONSUMERS
Year: 2004
North America 30.1%
Pacific-Asia 28.8%
Europe and Eurasia 25.9%
Africa 3.3%
Middle East 5.9%
Central and South America 6.0%
North America and Pacific-Asia account for 90 percent of the increase in petroleum consumption over the last 10 years.

Radioactive Minerals

Uranium and plutonium were used for the first time—for military purposes—in the 1940s. Once World War II ended, nuclear reactors and their fuels began to be used as sources of energy. To process these minerals, nuclear plants are necessary. They must be built following many safety guidelines, since nuclear energy is considered to be very risky. Accidents like the one in Chernobyl and, more recently, in Tokaimura, Japan, are clear examples of what can happen when control of this form of energy is lost. These images show the structure and heart of a nuclear reactor, the way uranium is processed, and the peaceful uses of this type of energy.

Pressure Vessel

The nuclear reactor is inserted into a vessel formed by steel that is approximately 1.6 feet (0.5 m) thick. The fuel, which is encapsulated in zirconium alloy sheaths, is located inside the hollow space of the vessel. This design helps to meet one of the first goals in nuclear safety: to prevent radioactive products from leaking into the surrounding environment.

URANIUM HANDLING

Uranium 235 is the only isotope that is found in a natural state, easily fissionable. For this reason, it is the main fuel used in nuclear power plants. Even though it is rare to find it in the Earth's crust, it can be found in enriching deposits in watercourse beds.

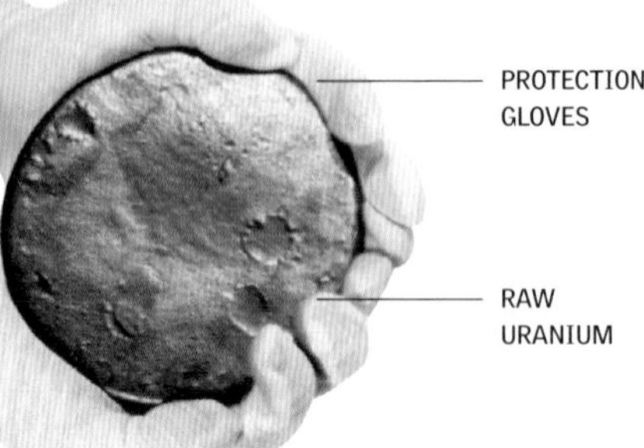

PROTECTION GLOVES

RAW URANIUM

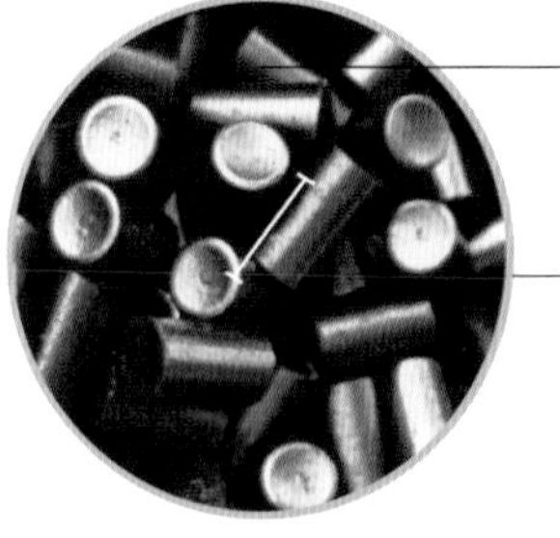

URANIUM PELLETS FOR USE IN A FUEL ROD

GROUPS OF FUEL RODS THAT GENERATE THE NUCLEAR REACTION

264
FUEL RODS IN EACH GROUP

THE NUCLEUS OF THE REACTOR

is in the lower part of the safety vessel, in which there are about 200 groups of fuel sheaths sized 0.4 inch (1 cm) in diameter and 13 feet (4 m) in height.

572° F
(300° C)
THE TEMPERATURE OF THE WATER PELLET

CONTROL RODS

MACHINERY ROOM

PIPING TUNNEL

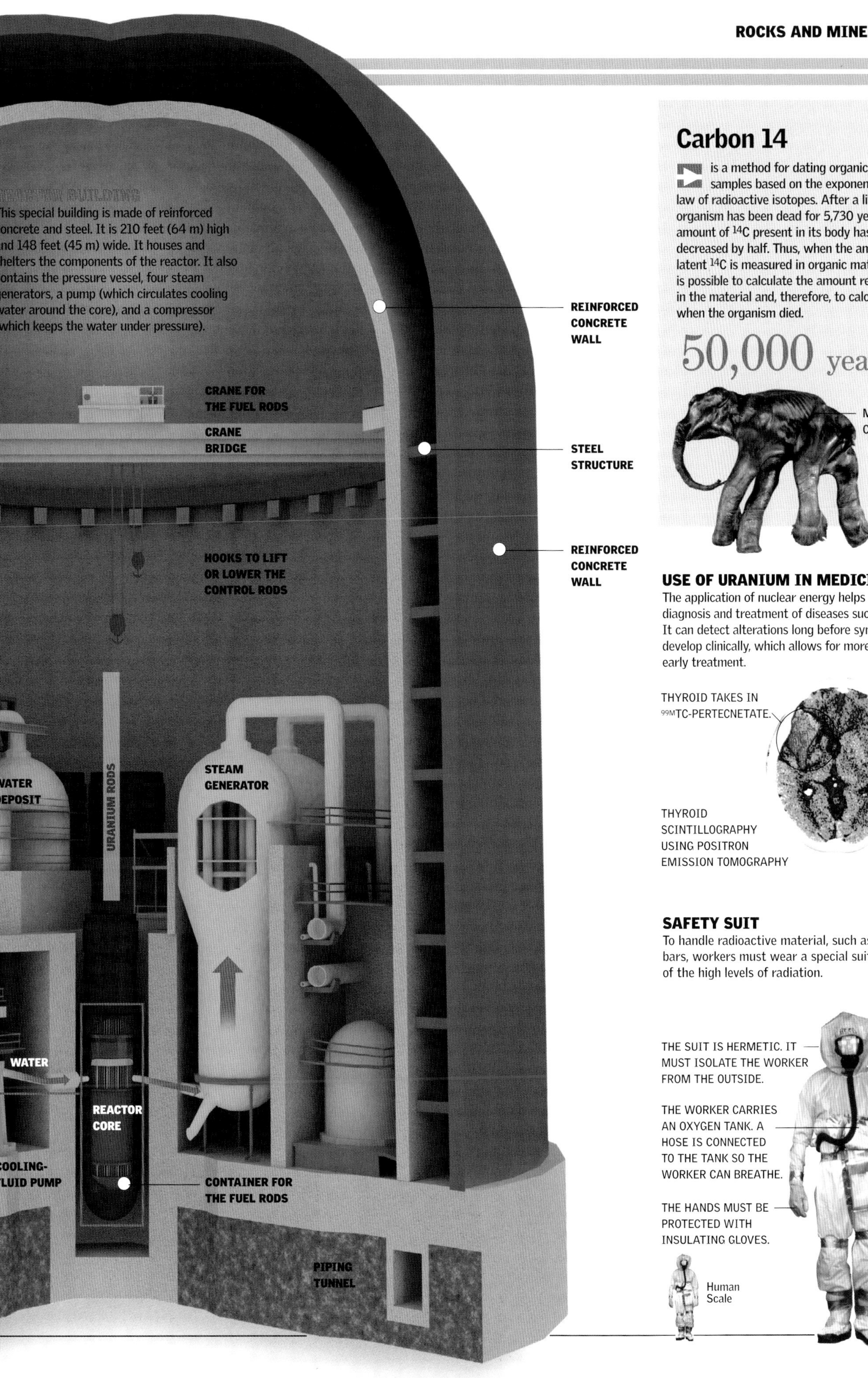

Carbon 14

is a method for dating organic fossil samples based on the exponential decay law of radioactive isotopes. After a living organism has been dead for 5,730 years, the amount of ^{14}C present in its body has decreased by half. Thus, when the amount of latent ^{14}C is measured in organic materials, it is possible to calculate the amount remaining in the material and, therefore, to calculate when the organism died.

50,000 years

MAMMOTH CUB

USE OF URANIUM IN MEDICINE

The application of nuclear energy helps with the diagnosis and treatment of diseases such as cancer. It can detect alterations long before symptoms develop clinically, which allows for more effective early treatment.

THYROID TAKES IN ^{99M}TC-PERTECNETATE.

THYROID SCINTILLOGRAPHY USING POSITRON EMISSION TOMOGRAPHY

SAFETY SUIT

To handle radioactive material, such as spent fuel bars, workers must wear a special suit because of the high levels of radiation.

THE SUIT IS HERMETIC. IT MUST ISOLATE THE WORKER FROM THE OUTSIDE.

THE WORKER CARRIES AN OXYGEN TANK. A HOSE IS CONNECTED TO THE TANK SO THE WORKER CAN BREATHE.

THE HANDS MUST BE PROTECTED WITH INSULATING GLOVES.

Human Scale

Glossary

Alkalines

Minerals that have a high content of potassium, sodium, lithium, rubidium, and calcium.

Amorphous

Mineral with fractured surfaces instead of crystalline faces. Noncrystalline.

Anticline

A fold of sedimentary strata sloping upwards like an arch.

Asthenosphere

Layer inside the Earth, below the lithosphere. It is part of the upper mantle and is composed of easily deformable rock.

Atom

The smallest unit of matter.

Bacteria

Microscopic and unicellular life-form found in air, water, plants, animals, and on the Earth's crust.

Batholith

Great mass (larger than 60 square miles [100 sq km] of surface) of intrusive igneous rocks.

Bravais Lattices

Three-dimensional crystal systems, based on certain mathematical principles, that represent the 14 types of cell units.

Butte

Hill with a flat top and sloping sides, found in areas that have undergone intense erosion.

Canyon

Deep, narrow valley formed by fluvial erosion.

Carat

Unit of weight used in jewelry, variable in time and place, equivalent to 0.007 ounce (0.2 g).

Cave

Subterranean cavity formed through the chemical action of water on soluble, generally calcareous, ground.

Cementation

Process by which sediment both loses porosity and is lithified through the chemical precipitation of material in the spaces between the grains.

Cementation Zone

Place where lithification occurs. Water infiltrates the area, fills up the spaces between the grains of sediment, and transforms loose sediment into a solid mass.

Chasm, or Rift

Wide valley formed as a consequence of the extension of the crust at the boundaries of diverging tectonic plates.

Chemical Compound

Substance formed by more than one element.

Chemical Element

Substance that contains only one type of atom.

Clay

Fine-grained sediments formed by the chemical decomposition of some rocks. It is malleable when wet and hardens as it dries.

Coal

Combustible black rock of organic origin. It is produced through the decomposition of plant materials that accumulate in swamps or shallow marine waters.

Concretion

Hard mass of mineral material that usually holds a fossil inside.

Contact Metamorphism

Large-scale transformation of a rock into another type of rock. This happens mostly as a consequence of a sudden temperature increase.

Convection Currents

Moving pathways of material that occur inside the mantle as a consequence of the transfer of heat coming from the Earth's core. The hottest zones of the mantle rise, and the coldest ones sink. These movements are probably responsible for the movement of tectonic plates.

Crack

Fissure or cavity in the rock that results from tension. It can be completely or partially filled with minerals.

Crust

External layer of the Earth. There are two types of crust: continental crust forms large terrestrial masses, and oceanic crust forms the bottoms of the oceans.

Crystal

Organized, regular, and periodically repeated arrangement of atoms.

Crystalline System

It includes all crystals that can be related to the same set of symmetric elements.

Density

Amount of mass of a mineral per unit of volume.

Deposit

A natural accumulation of a rock or mineral. If it is located at the site where it formed, the deposit is called primary. Otherwise, it is called secondary.

Diatomite

Light, porous rock. It has a light color, and it is consolidated. Composed exclusively (or almost) of diatoms.

Dolostone

Carbonated sedimentary rock that contains at least 50 percent or more carbonate, of which at least half appears as dolomite.

Earthquake

The sudden and violent release of energy and vibrations in the Earth that generally occurs along the edges of tectonic plates.

Elasticity

Tendency of a mineral to recover its shape after being subjected to flexion or torsion.

Era

Division of time in the Earth's history. Geologists divide eras into periods.

Erosion

Removal and transport of sediment through the action of water, ice, and wind.

Evaporation

Process through which a liquid becomes gas without boiling.

Exfoliation

The tendency for certain minerals to fracture along regular planes within their crystalline structure.

Fault

Fracture involving the shifting of one rock mass with respect to another.

Flexibility

Ability of minerals to bend without fracturing.

Fluorescence

Property of some minerals that enables them to emit a certain level of light when exposed to ultraviolet rays. The fluorescent properties present in a metal can make it look as if it were truly fluorescent.

Fold

Bending and deformation of rock strata due to the compression caused by the movements of tectonic plates.

Fossil

Any trace of an old life-form. It can be the petrified remains of an organism or an impression of an organism left in rock.

Fossil Fuel

Fuel formed from the partially decomposed remains of deceased organisms. These mixtures of organic compounds are extracted from the subsoil with the goal of producing energy through combustion. They are coal, oil, and natural gas.

Fracture

Break of a mineral along an irregular surface. It can be conchoidal, hooked, smooth, or earthy.

Gem

Mineral or other natural material that is valued for its beauty and rarity. It can be polished and cut to produce jewels.

Geode

Spherical, rocky cavity covered with well-formed crystals.

Geology

Study of the Earth, its shape, and its composition. Rocks, minerals, and fossils offer information that helps us reconstruct the history of the planet.

Glacier

A large mass of ice formed through the accumulation of recrystallized and compacted snow occurring either on a mountain or over a large area on a landmass. Ice moves slowly and both excavates rock and carries debris.

Granite

Intrusive igneous rock composed mainly of quartz and feldspar. It can be polished and used in decoration.

Habit

External aspect of a crystal that reflects its predominant shape.

Hardness

Resistance offered by a mineral to scratching and abrasion. One mineral is said to be harder than another if the former can scratch the latter.

Hot Spot

Place within a tectonic plate where active volcanoes form.

Hydrothermal

Process involving the physical and chemical transformations suffered by rocks or minerals through the action of hot fluids (water and gases) associated with a magma body.

Igneous Rocks

Rocks formed directly from the cooling of magma. If they solidify inside the crust, they are said to be plutonic (or intrusive); if they solidify on the surface, they are said to be volcanic (or extrusive).

Impermeable Rock

Rock through which liquids cannot be filtered.

Intrusion

A large mass of rock that forms in empty spaces underground when magma infiltrates strata, cools, and solidifies.

Jade

White or green metamorphic rock formed by a compact and tenacious filter of very fine needles of tremolite. It is a rare rock used in art objects.

Karst Cycle

Formation cycle of caves that lasts a total of about one million years.

Kimberlite

Type of rock usually associated with diamonds and other minerals coming from the depths of the Earth.

Lava

Magma expelled on the surface of the Earth.

Limestone

Rock containing at least 50% calcite. It can also have dolomite, aragonite, and siderite.

Lithosphere

Exterior, rigid layer of the Earth formed by the crust and upper mantle.

Lode

Sub-superficial rock intrusion of tabular-shaped rock.

Luster

Level of light reflection on the surface of a crystal.

Magma

Hot, rocky material from the crust and upper mantle in liquid state that forms crystals as it cools. When magma is expelled at the Earth's surface, it is called lava.

Magmatic Rock

Rock that forms when magma cools off and solidifies. Magmatic intrusive rocks solidify underground, while the extrusive ones solidify on the surface.

Magnetism

Property of some minerals that allows them to be attracted by a magnet and to change the direction of a compass needle.

Malleability

Mechanical property of a mineral that makes it possible for the mineral to be molded and formed into a sheet through repeated blows without breaking.

Mantle

The layer between the crust and external core. It includes the upper mantle and lower mantle.

Marble

Metamorphosed limestone rock composed of compacted calcite and dolomite. It can be polished.

Massive

One of the possible habits of a consistent mineral that refers to the tendency for certain crystals to intertwine and form a solid mass rather than independent crystals.

Metal

Any element that shines, conducts electricity, and is malleable.

Metamorphic Rock

Type of rock resulting from the application of high pressure and temperature on igneous and sedimentary rocks.

Mineral

Inorganic solid of natural origin that has an organized atomic structure.

Mohs Scale

A tool designed to test the hardness of a given mineral by comparing it to 10 known minerals, from the softest to the hardest. Each mineral can be scratched by those following it.

Molecule

Chemical compound formed when one or several types of atoms are joined together.

Native Element

An element that occurs in nature that is not combined with other elements. Sulfur and gold are examples of native elements.

Oceanic Trench

Narrow and deep submarine depression formed when the oceanic crust of one tectonic plate moves beneath another.

Ornamental Stone

It is not a precious stone, but it can be used in jewelry or for other ornamental purposes.

Outcrop

Part of a rock formation devoid of vegetation or soil that stands out from the Earth's surface.

Oxidation Zone

Deposit of minerals with oxidizing properties, formed through the effect of meteorization or weathering.

Petrifaction

Cell-by-cell replacement of organic matter, such as bones or wood, with minerals of the surrounding solutions.

Piezoelectric

Property that some minerals have to produce a difference in potential when subjected to compression, traction, or torsion.

Placer

Mineral concentrations as deposits of placer during time lapses that vary from a few decades up to millions of years.

Pyroelectric

Property that some nonconductor minerals have to create difference in power transmissions from differences in temperature.

Quartzite

Metamorphic rock formed by the consolidation of quartz sandstone. It is extremely hard. Quartzite can also be a sedimentary rock, which is sandstone with a very high content of quartz; it is very hard and it has light color.

Regional Metamorphism

Metamorphism occurring in rock over large areas.

Rock

Natural aggregate of one or more minerals (sometimes including noncrystalline substances) that constitute an independent geologic unit.

Sedimentary Rock

Rock that forms through accumulation of sediments that, when subjected to physical and chemical processes, result in a compacted and consolidated material. Sediment can form on river banks, at the bottom of precipices, in valleys, lakes, and seas. Sedimentary rock accumulates in successive layers, or strata.

Sediments

Rock fragments or remains of plants or animals deposited at the bottom of rivers, lakes, or oceans by water, wind, or ice.

Seismic Waves

Elastic waves that travel through the Earth after an earthquake. They can also be produced artificially through explosions.

Silicates

They make up about 95 percent of the Earth's crust. Their tetrahedral structure, with one silicon and four oxygen ions, creates different types of configurations through the union of the ions. According to their composition, members of this mineral group are differentiated into light and dark.

Slate

Bluish black, fine-grained metamorphic rock. It can be easily divided into sheets.

Solution

Mixture of two or more chemical substances. It can be liquid, solid, or gaseous.

Stalactite

Internal structure of a cave. It is conical and hangs from the cave ceiling.

Stalagmite

Internal structure of a cave. It is conical and rises from the cave floor.

Streak

Characteristic color of the fine dust obtained from a mineral by rubbing it over an unglazed porcelain plate.

Streak Test

A test that involves rubbing a mineral against an unglazed white porcelain sheet to obtain dust. The color of the dust left on the tile can help identify the mineral.

Symmetry Axes

Symmetry element that enables the repetition of crystalline faces to form different shapes.

Syncline

Concave fold of sedimentary rock strata. The younger rocks are located at the center of the concave.

Talus Slope

Accumulation of fragments resulting from the mechanical weathering of rocks. The sediment deposit forms more or less in situ as the result of the transport of materials through gravity over a small distance.

Tectonic Elevation

Rising of rocks as a consequence of the movements of tectonic plates.

Tectonic Plates

Rigid fragments of the lithosphere that move on the asthenosphere.

Tenacity

The level of toughness that a mineral offers to fracture, deformation, crushing, bending, or pulverization.

Transparent

It is said that a mineral is clear when light goes through it without weakening. When only some light passes through, the mineral is called translucent. If no light passes through, it is called opaque.

Vein

Fracture that cuts through rocks and is filled by some mineral.

Volcanic Outcropping

Isolated pile of hard magmatic rocks that remain after the disappearance of the rest of the volcano due to erosion.

Weathering

The breaking down of a material by sustained physical or chemical processes.

Index

A

abrasion platform, 49
agate, 23
 crystallizing pattern, 43
Alexander the Great, Valley of Diamonds, 35
allochromatic mineral, 22
Allosaurus, 10
alloy, 39
Alps, formation, 10
aluminum, 79
amethyst, 22
 color, 33
ammonia, covalent bond, 28
ammonite, extinction, 10
Andes mountain range, formation, 11
angiosperm, 10
anhydrite, 39
anion, 28
anthracite, 71
apatite, 38
 hardness, 24
Appalachian Mountains, formation, 9
aragonite, chemical crystallization, 21
Argentina, Veladero mine, 80-81
arkose (sandstone), 69
ash cone, 43
Asscher, Joseph, 35
asthenosphere (Earth's mantle), 11
atom, crystalline structures, 28, 29
augite, 36
aureole, 55
Australia, Uluru-Kata Tjuta National Park, 58-59
automobile: *See* **car**
Ayers, Henry, 59
Ayers Rock (Australia): *See* **Uluru-Kata Tjuta National Park**

B

Baltica, Ural Mountains formation, 9
barytine, 39
basalt, 43
 eruptions, 9
 formation, 12, 65
batholith, 16, 42, 43
 Yosemite National Park, 44
bauxite, 38
beach, formation, 49
bedrock, 57
Bering Strait, modern humans, 11
Bingham Canyon (Utah, United States), 82-83
biotite, 37
birefringent mineral, 23
bismuth, 20
Black Stone of the Ka'bah (Mecca, Saudi Arabia), 59
blackboard chalk, 68
Borena (ethnic group), 27
Bowen's reaction series, 43
Bravais, Auguste, 30
Bravais lattices, 30
brazilianite, crystalline system, 30
breccia, 69
Bridal Veil Falls (Yosemite National Park, United States), 45
Burkhardt, Jean L., 74

C

calcite, 66
 chemical crystallization, 21
 hardness, 24
calcium sulfate, 39
caldera, 43
Caledonian range, 9
California (United States), gold rush, 84-85
Cambrian explosion, 9
Cambrian Period, 9
Cango Caves (South Africa), 50-51
canyon
 Bingham Canyon, 82-83
 formation, 46, 51
 Grand Canyon, 52-53, 66
car, elements, 78-79
carbon, mineral structure, 21
carbon-14 dating, 53, 91
carbonate, 39
Carboniferous Period, 9
carbonization, 70
cascades, 45
cataclasite, formation, 54
Cathedral Rocks (Yosemite National Park, United States), 45
cation, 28
cave, 50-51
 Australian Aborigine paintings, 59
 formation, 49
 Neversink Pit, 40-41
cementation (sedimentary rock), 49, 69
Cenozoic Era, 10-11
Central Rocky Mountains (United States),
formation, 10
chalcopyrite, 38
chalk, 68
chemical element, 8, 16, 20
chemical weathering process, 15
Chicxulub (Mexico), meteor impact, 10
Chile, Torres del Paine National Park, 16-17
citrine, 22
clast, detrital rocks, 68
clay
 kaoline, 68
 lutite, 68
 structure, 36
cliff, formation, 49
coal
 deposits, 71, 77
 formation, 70-71
 mining, 76-77, 86-87
coastal drift, 4
coastal plain, 49
color
 mineral, 22: *See also* **streak color**
 rock, 63
column (cave structure), 50
compaction (sedimentary rock), 49
compound mineral, 20

conglomerate (sedimentary rock), 69
contact metamorphism, 55
  See also **metamorphism**
copper, 38
  mining, 82-83
coquina, 66
coral reef, 66-67
Corkscrew Canyon (Arizona, United States), 6-7, 14-15
corundum, hardness, 25
covalent bond, 28
Cretaceous Period, 10
crystal
  atomic model, 29
  Bravais lattices, 30
  characterization, 30
  crystallographic axes, 31
  crystallographic chemistry, 28
  formation, 63
  internal network, 29
  precious stones, 32
crystalline network, categorization, 30
crystalline system, 30-31
crystallization system, 21
crystallographic axis, 31
crystallographic chemistry, 28
crystallography, 28
cubic crystalline system, 30
Cullinan diamond, 35

D

Dallol volcano (Ethiopia), 18-19, 26-27
deflation, geologic processes, 46
delta, formation, 48
dendrite, 38
density (mineral), 25
desert, 46
desertic soil, 56
detrital rock, 68-69
Devonian Period, 9
diamond, 19, 32-33
  cuts, 33
  hardness, 21, 25
  history, 34-35
  structure, 21, 30, 33
dike, 42, 43, 65
dinosaur, mass extinctions, 10
dolomite, 66
dune, erosion, 46
dynamic metamorphism, 54
  See also **metamorphism**

E

Earth
  history, 4-5, 8-9
  layers, 11
earthquake, causes, 13
Earth's core, 9, 11, 42
Earth's crust, 8, 11, 42
Earth's mantle, 11, 42
earthworm, humus production, 57
Ediacaran fauna, 8
effusive rock, formation, 12
Egyptian iconography, 75
El Capitan (Yosemite National Park, United States), 44
electric current, 25
element, chemical, 8, 16, 20
emerald, color, 32
Eocene Epoch, 10
eolian process (erosion), 14
erosion, 14, 46
  rock formation: *See* **sedimentary rock**
  soil formation, 57
erratics, glaciers, 47
estuary, 49
Ethiopia
  Borena ethnic group, 27
  Dallol volcano, 18-19, 26-27
  volcanic cave house, 4-5
exfoliation, 24, 63
exotic mineral, quartz color, 22
extended cave system, 50
Externsteine rock formation (Germany), 58
extinction: *See* **mass extinction**
extrusive rock (volcanic rock), 65
  formation, 12, 42, 43
  rock cycle, 57

F

fault (rock fracture), 13
feldspar, 17
fissure, granite rock, 45
flowering plant, Cretaceous Period, 10
fluorite, 39
  hardness, 24
foliation, 72
fool's gold: *See* **pyrite**
fossil
  Cambrian explosion, 9
  dating, 53, 91
  formation, 53
  hominid, 11
  succession, 52, 53
fractional distillation, 89
fracture, 13, 24, 63
  temperature effects, 15
Fugitive Slave Law, 84
fusion (rock), 55

G

gabbro (rock), 64
galena, structure, 21
garnet, color, 33
garnetiferous schist, 72-73
gas: *See* **petroleum**
gem (precious stone), 18-19, 32-33
geode, 60, 61
geologic process: *See* **erosion; weathering**

geologic time scale, 8-11
rock layers, 53
geology, branches, 16
Germany, Externsteine rock formation, 58
Giant's Causeway (Northern Ireland), 65
glacial cirque, 47
glaciation
Precambrian Period, 8
Quaternary Period, 11
glacier, 44, 47, 56
glass, atomic model, 29
gneiss, 72
formation, 9, 55
metamorphism, 73
gold
gold rush, 84-85
metals, 20
mining, 80-81
Gondwana (continent), 9
grain (rock), 63
Grand Canyon (United States), 52-53, 66
granite, 12, 17, 42, 44, 45, 64
granodiorite, 64
graphite
chemical crystallization, 21
hardness, 21
use, 19
Yosemite National Park, 44-45
graywacke, 69
Great Koh-I-Noor diamond, 34
Great Star of Africa diamond, 35
Greece, ancient, architecture in Petra, 75
gypsum, 39
hardness, 24
use, 19

H

Hadean Era, 8
Half Dome (Yosemite National Park, United States), 45
halide, 39
halite: *See* **salt**
hardness (mineral)
diamond, 21
graphite, 21
Mohs scale, 21, 24
quartzite, 73
hematite, 23
hexagonal crystalline system, 30
Himalayas (Asia), formation, 10
Holocene Epoch, 11
Hope Diamond, 35
hopper (mining equipment), 85
hornblende schist, 72
hornito (salt formation), 26, 27
human being, emergence, 11
humus, 57
hydraulic mining, 85
hydrocarbon, 78
hydrologic process, erosion, 14
hydroxide, 38

I

idiochromatic mineral, 22
igneous rock, 64-65
formation, 42-43
rock cycle, 57
immigrant labor, gold mining, 84
India, diamond history, 34, 35
inselberg, 46
internal geodynamics, 12
intrusive rock (plutonic rock), 64
formation, 12, 42
rock cycle, 57
ionic bond, 28
iron, 79
isomorphism, 21

J-K

joint (rock fracture), 13
Jordan, Petra, 74-75
Jurassic Period, 10
kaoline, 68
See also **clay**
kaolinite, 36
karst cycle, 50
Kilauea Crater (Hawaii, United States), 12-13
Kimberley mine, 32
Koh-I-Noor diamond, Great, 34

L

labradorite, 31
laccolith, 43
laterite soil, 56
lava, 43
leaching (lixiviation), 82
lignite, 71
limestone, 68
Externsteine formation, 58
formation, 66
karst cycle, 50
Neversink Pit, 40-41
stalactite formation, 51
limolite: *See* **limestone**
limonite, 38
lithosphere, 11
lixiviation (leaching), 82
luminescence, 23
luster, 23
pearl, 67
lutite, 68

M

magma, rock formation, 42, 43
  See also **igneous rock; volcanic rock**
magmatism, 12
magnesite, structure, 21
magnesium, 78, 79
magnetite, 38
malachite, 22, 39
mammal, Cenozoic Era, 10-11
mammoth, 11, 91
marble, 73
  colors, 63
marcasite, chemical crystallization, 21
mass extinction
  Cretaceous Period, 10
  Permian Period, 9
Mauna Loa volcano (Hawaii, United States), 12-13
McLean, Evelyn Walsh, 35
Mecca (Saudi Arabia), Black Stone of the Ka'bah, 59
mechanical weathering process, 15
Mesozoic Era, 10
metal
  car parts, 78-79
  luster, 23
  native minerals, 21, 22
metamorphic rock, 12
  classification, 72
  rock cycle, 57
metamorphism, 12, 54-55
meteor, Yucatán Peninsula, 10
Mexico, Yucatán Peninsula meteor, 10
mica, 17
micaceous schist, 72
mineral, 18-39
  chemical perspective, 17
  classification, 20-23
  optical property, 22-23
  physical properties, 24-25
  radioactive, 90-91
  sources, 5
  structure, 21
mineralization process, Dallol volcano, 26
mining
  coal, 76-77, 86-87
  copper, 82-83
  gold, 80-81, 84-85
  hydraulic, 85
  open-air mine, 82-83
  silver, 80-81
  types, 82
Miocene Epoch, 11
Mohs, Friedrich, 24
Mohs scale of hardness, 24-25
  diamonds, 21
  graphite, 21
monoclinic crystalline system, 30
monorefringent mineral, 23
moraine, 47
mother-of-pearl, 67
mountain
  formation, 9, 10, 11, 13
  See also specific names, for example **Sierra Nevada range**
Mountain of Light (diamond): *See* **Great Koh-I-Noor diamond**
mylonite, formation, 54

N

Nabataean people, Petra, 74-75
native mineral, 20
Neversink Pit (Alabama, United States), 40-41
nonmetal mineral, 20, 38
  car parts, 79
  luster, 23
nonsilicate mineral, 38-39
Northern Ireland, Giant's Causeway, 65
nuclear energy, 77, 90-91
nuclear reactor, 90-91

obsidian, 43, 65
ocean
  first, 8
  marine sediments, 66-67
Oligocene Epoch, 11
olivine, 36
opal, 32
open-air mine, 82-83
optical property (mineral), 22-23
Ordovician Period, 9
organic rock, 61, 70
original horizontality principle, 53
orogeny, 9
orthoclase, hardness, 25
oxide, 38

Paleocene Epoch, 10
Paleozoic Era, 9
  calcareous formations, 66
Pangea (continent), 9
Panotia (supercontinent), 9
Patagonia, formation, 11
pearl, formation, 67
peat bog, coal formation, 70
pegmatite, 65
peridotite, 64
permafrost, 56
Permian Period, 9
Petra (Jordan), 74-75
petrographic microscope, 22
petroleum (gas)
  combustion, 78
  formation and reserves, 70-71
  production process, 88-89
phosphate, 38
phraetic layer, mining, 83
phyllite, formation, 54, 72

piezoelectricity, 25
Pleistocene Epoch, 11
Pliocene Epoch, 11
plutonic rock (intrusive rock), 64
formation, 12, 42
rock cycle, 57
polymorphism, 21
porphyritic rock, 65
positron emission tomography, 91
Precambrian Period, 8
precious stone, colors, 32-33
See also specific types, for example **diamond**
pressure, effect on rock structure, 55
prism, 30
Giant's Causeway, 65
Proterozoic Era, 8
pumice, 65
pyrite (fool's gold)
chemical crystallization, 21
structure, 39
pyroclastic material: *See* **volcanic ash**
pyroelectricity, 25
Quaternary Period, 11
quartz
agate, 23
color, 22
composition, 17
hardness, 25
structure, 37
quartzite, 73

R

radioactive mineral, 90-91
ranker (soil type), 56
rapids, 48
refining, petroleum, 89
refraction, 23
regional metamorphism, 55
See also **metamorphism**
reptile
Cretaceous Period extinction, 10
Mesozoic Era, 10
rhodochrosite, 31
rhombic crystalline system, 31
river, sediment transportation, 48-49
rock, 60-75
color, 62
formation, 16-17, 62
identification, 62-63
mineralogical composition, 62
shape, 62
transformation: *See* **metamorphism**
See also specific types, for example **granite**
rock crystal, 22
rock cycle, 6-7, 57
Rocky Mountains (North America), formation, 10
Rodinia (early supercontinent), 8
rose quartz, 22
ruby, color, 32

S

safety measure, radioactive material, 90, 91
salt (halite), 19, 20
extraction, 27
ionic bond, 28
structure, 21, 28-29
salt deposit, hornito formation, 27
sandstone
classification, 69
Petra, 74-75
Uluru, 58-59
sapphire, color, 33
Saudi Arabia, Black Stone of the Ka'bah, 59
scheelite, 31
schist, 55
types, 72-73
Scotland, gneiss formation, 9, 54-55
sediment
soil formation, 56
water transportation, 48-49
wind transportation, 47
sedimentary rock
detrital rock, 68-69
formation, 46-49, 57
marine organic remains, 66-67
See also **stalactite; stalagmite**
sedimentation, 15, 48
semimetal mineral, 20
semiprecious stone
color, 33
See also **precious stone**
Serapis (Egyptian god), 75
Siberia, Ural Mountains formation, 9
siderite, structure, 21
Sierra Nevada range (United States), 44-45
silicate, structures, 29, 36-37
silicon, 79
sill (rock formation), 42, 65
Silurian Period, 9
silver
crystal dendrite, 20
mining, 80-81
sinkhole, 50
slate, 39, 72
formation, 9
micrography, 72
phyllite formation, 54, 72
sluice box, 85
Smithsonian Institution, Hope Diamond, 35
smoky quartz, 22
soil
formation, 56
humus, 57
profile, 57
types, 56
South Africa
Cango Caves, 50-51
diamonds, 35
stalactite, 50
formation, 51
stalagmite, 50
stock (rock formation), 43
streak color, 23
See also **color**

stripe (rock), 72
subsoil, 57
sulfate, 39
sulfide, 39
sulfur, 19, 20, 22
supercontinent, 8, 9

T

talc, 37
  hardness, 24
Taylor, Elizabeth, 35
Taylor-Burton diamond, 35
temperature, degree of metamorphism, 55
terminal moraine, 47
Tertiary Period, 10-11
tetragonal crystalline system, 31
texture (rock), 63
thyroid, scintillography, 91
till, glaciers, 47
topaz, 31
  color, 33
  hardness, 25
Torres del Paine National Park (Chile), 16-17
tourmaline, 24-25
transportation, eroded materials, 15
Triassic Period, 10
triclinic crystalline system, 31
trigonal crystalline system, 31
trilobite, 9, 52
tropics, laterite soil, 56
tuff, detrital rocks, 68
tunnel, formation, 51
turquoise, color, 33

U

Uluru-Kata Tjuta National Park (Australia), 58-59
unconformity, rock layers, 53
United Kingdom
  Giant's Causeway, 65
  royal family's diamond ownership, 34, 35
United States of America
  Bingham Canyon, 82-83
  Corkscrew Canyon, 6-7, 14-15
  gold mining, 84-85
  Grand Canyon, 52-53, 66
  Mauna Loa volcano, 12-13
  Neversink Pit, 40-41
  Yosemite National Park, 44-45
Ural Mountains (Eurasia), formation, 9
uranium, 77
  handling, 90
  medical uses, 91

V

Valley of Diamonds (legend), 35
vanadinite, 30
Veladero mine (Argentina), 80-81
Victoria, Queen, Great Koh-I-Noor diamond, 34
volcanic ash, 68
  ash cone, 43
volcanic rock (extrusive rock), 65
  formation, 12, 42, 43
  rock cycle, 57
volcano
  caldera, 43
  Dallol, 18-19, 26-27
  Mauna Loa 12-13
  rock formation, 42, 65

water
  cave formation, 50-51
  erosion, 14
  hornitos, 26, 27
  sediment transportation, 48-49
  weathering, 15
waterfall
  formation, 48
  Yosemite National Park, 45
weathering, 14, 15
wind
  deserts, 46
  erosion, 14
  sediment transportation, 47
Winston, Harry, 35

X-Z

X-ray diffraction, 22
  crystal structure identification, 28
Yosemite National Park (United States), 44-45
Yucatán Peninsula (Mexico), meteor, 10
zooxanthellae, coral reefs, 67